The Image Factor

A Guide
to
Effective
Self-
Presentation
for
Career
Enhancement

Eleri Sampson

KOGAN
PAGE

First published in 1994, reprinted 1995

Kogan Page Limited
120 Pentonville Road
London N1 9JN

© Eleri Sampson 1994

British Library Cataloguing in Publication Data

A CIP record for this book is available from the British Library.

ISBN 0-7494-1210-0

Typeset by Books Unlimited (Nottm), Sutton-in-Ashfield NG17 1AL

Printed and bound in Great Britain by Biddles Limited, Guildford and King's Lynn

The
Image
Factor

The ~~~ ~~ ~~ ~~ ~~ned o~ o~ ~efor~

CONTENTS

ACKNOWLEDGEMENTS

Thank you to Paperlink and the artist Steve Best for permission to use the 'Bestie' cartoon on page 103.

Thank you to the Springboard organisation and the cartoonist Viv Quillan for the use of the cartoon on page 40.

My special thanks to my family, friends, colleagues and clients for their interest and support and very special thanks to my partner Alan Felton.

CHAPTER

WHAT IS THE IMAGE FACTOR?

The image factor is the extent to which personal image and operational style influence internal promotion or external appointment.

Working hard, being conscientious and reliable and turning up on time are not going to get you promoted, because doing a good job is simply what you get paid for. Personal image, management style and visibility are the things that will make the difference to how far you get and how well you get on in an organization. Careers are now the responsibility of the individual, not the organization. Dynamic organizations can provide an arena for employees to display their talents rather than offer a job for life in return for loyalty and services rendered. This book is aimed at anyone willing to take charge of their career development and demonstrates how personal style and professional image can have a powerful influence on career development. It combines insights from behavioural psychology with down-to-earth advice, self-completing exercises and case studies.

PERSONAL IMAGE AND ORGANIZATIONAL CULTURE

The Image Factor uses the knowledge I have gained about what makes people tick, what motivates them and what holds them back professionally because of their perceptions about themselves and about organizational cultures. Knowing where to market yourself is as important as developing yourself into a marketable product. I meet many different professionals — senior executives, middle managers, their employers and employees in both the public and private sectors, from one person operated businesses to multi-national corporations — all with a view about the significance of personal image. Insights have been gained from meeting a wide range of people through workshops, seminars, coaching programmes and daily contact with professional people in business. The following information is intended for managers in work who want to develop their career upwards or sideways. It can also be used by those who are out of work and actively job seeking.

Managers need an 'extra edge' if they are to succeed. All management is in the end about managing people. People are persuaded by personal style, professionalism, charisma. Managers need to communicate their personal style — what they stand for and what the organization stands for — to colleagues, clients and competitors. They need to get their message across consistently and effectively every day of their working lives — all this without compromising their principles, without going under and somehow retaining their identity and their sense of humour. They need support and some sensible, practical advice and some tricks of the trade. This is what *The Image Factor* is all about.

Your image takes on reality only when it has an audience to respond to it, even if it is only an audience of one. The potential audience is vast — the whole of the world of work. The response to your image and personal style will vary according to where the work you do is positioned on the map. There is a sophisticated mix between the way an organization conducts its business and the nature of its business. An organization can be perceived as 'conservative' or 'creative'. Although they might be considered stereotypical, style associations are frequently made along these lines:

Conservative	**Creative**
• doing things the traditional way	• innovative
• in favour of the status quo	• change
• rule bound	• free structure
• 'old'	• 'new'
• slow	• fast
• autocratic	• democratic

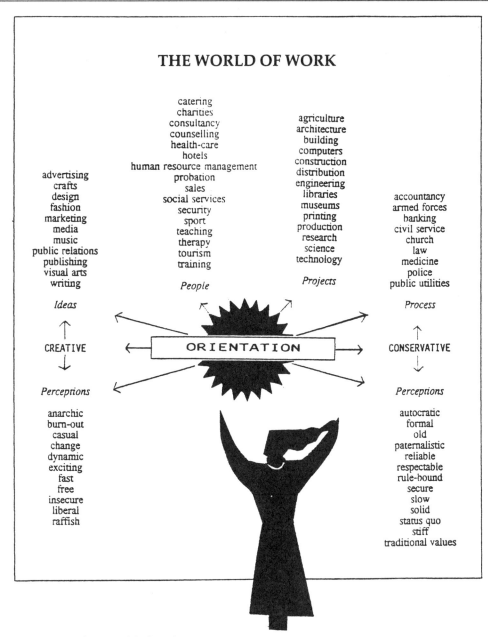

Figure 1.1 *Map of the world of work*

You need to establish where your personal style will fit best. For example, a well established chartered accountancy firm will fit firmly into the 'conservative' style and partners will reflect that style in order to meet the expectations of traditional clients, who form the bulk of their business. The stereotype could be broken by a marketing manager in the same firm who, by contrast, could have a flamboyant and creative style associated with the sales and presentation function.

Business orientation

Organizations can be said to be 'people', 'process' or 'ideas' orientated. Some organizations are so huge that they represent the whole range of orientations across their departments and functions. Individuals are usually happiest when they can work within the orientation they prefer. Training is people orientated, yet I meet so many trainers who seem to dislike people and would really be happier writing training manuals. There are people involved in production and project development who need an audience. They need to motivate and inspire people, not machines. There are people involved in design or research who are barely house-trained and are wheeled out to meet clients, with disastrous results.

Role and function

Whatever the product or service delivered by the organization, any job can have a hands-on, management, strategic or support function. Do you actually do it? Manage it? Think and plan for it? Support other people doing it? Or a combination? Are you in a role that best displays your talent and experience?

In the limelight

Jobs have a front of curtain and backstage element. Laboratory research is a backstage role. Presenting that research to internal or external clients is a centre stage role. Have you got a clear idea of what you prefer? If you are ambitious, you need a job that places you front of curtain. Then with self-assurance and an appropriate personal image you will be correctly positioned to be noticed.

A perfect match

Like an actor, you are looking for the role of a lifetime. You are looking for the best possible match between your personal style, goals and ambitions and an organization's style, its ethics and the opportunities it can provide for you.

A picture of you

Understanding the significance of personal style comes from appreciating that everyone has an image. Your personal image is a picture of you. You can't not have an image! Whether you like it or not, what others see is what you have chosen to show them. What they see is a mixture of fixed and moveable assets. Your physical characteristics and temperament are inherited through your genes and to a certain degree are fixed. The way you walk, sit or stand are a result of training, temperament and conditioning, but the way you dress is a result of personal choice.

Accident, illness or constant conditioning can, of course, change what was there at birth. Being badly burnt in a car accident can leave you tragically scarred inside and out, resulting in psychological trauma and physical disfigurement. A bullying husband can constantly undermine a woman's confidence, limiting her choices about how she would prefer to look.

Within these constraints we all still have a choice about the way we look. Decisions about our appearance can speak volumes about who we think we are and what we stand for. You can't prevent other people from interpreting your look, so you might as well give them the impression you intended them to have.

WHAT IS AN IMAGE?

Think of your image as an advertisement. A picture on the outside advertising what is available on the inside. It is also a promise. A promise that the external image will deliver the skills, competences and values it advertises. Ask yourself exactly what it is that you want to tell people you are willing to deliver.

Everyone has certain principles by which they can be recognized. These principles should be evident from personal style. It is not just clothes that make an image. Personal image is a sophisticated mixture of internal and external factors that determine self-image, perceived image and required image.

This section is all about self-awareness. It is an important first step because when you are aware of the image you present you can set about marketing yourself with confidence. Taking charge of your self-development in this way is an adult thing to do and shows you already have a high level of self-regard.

Self-image

Self-image is influenced by past experience and is a reflection of our current level of self-esteem. On a good day the project you are managing is going really well, you are on target and within budget and you feel pleasantly plump. On a bad day when you don't get that job, the attractive and competent you becomes a fat slob who is always being rejected. How do you see yourself? What sort of person do you think you are? Do you see yourself as attractive, healthy, hardworking? Do you think of yourself as a success or a failure? Are you an introvert or an extrovert? What do you stand for? What do you like? What annoys you?

Exercise

Get a sheet of plain paper and at the top write your name in large letters. Give yourself 60 seconds and jot down any word or phrase that you think is typical of you. You can write anything at all that is about you. It can be to do with your temperament, behaviour, personality, likes and dislikes. Stop and read what you have written. Then give yourself another 2 minutes to refine or add to the list. All your qualities are important — the detail as well as the broad picture.

Use this brain-storming exercise as a basis for more considered thought at a later stage. When you feel confident about your strengths you can present them with assurance. Further exercises are given in Chapters 5 and 6. They can be tackled in different ways. For example, draw up two columns on a sheet of paper and head them 'strengths and weaknesses' or 'likes and dislikes' or 'assets and liabilities' or 'I can and I am'. The aim is to get to know yourself.

kind   reliable>*always keep my word*
perfectionist>*positive = high standards*
                 >*negative = high stress levels*
    loyal
likes music, likes sunshine, likes cats, likes food
   doesn't like noise and crowds
   well-dressed
earrings
nice legs
impatient> *doesn't suffer fools gladly*
      > *hates waiting for buses (or anything)*

Figure 1.2 *Self-image*

Perceived image

How do you know how you come across? One way is to listen to feedback, which can come in the form of either criticism or compliments.

Exercise

If you want to test how your image is perceived by others you could ask a friend, colleague or family member to do this exercise with you. Ask them to write down anything that comes to mind when they think of you. Remember that any quality can have its positive and negative interpretation; other people's view of you is still only their opinion. It is useful to ask for a second or third opinion and compare notes. You may find that this exercise shows up differences between the way you see yourself and the way others see you. It is possible you have no idea at all how others perceive you, in which case it's time to organize some feedback and give it some consideration. If you have rather a poor view of yourself you need to find some positive feedback to increase your self-image.

Received image – image and long distance reputation

People will often make judgements about others based on what they've heard, even before meeting them. They may base their judgement on what they think they know about a profession, a company or particular department and then extend it to include the individual. 'Architects are a funny lot...' or 'They're a law unto themselves in Sales – very difficult to work with...'

You can use your reputation, real or imagined, to your advantage. Suppose you have developed a reputation for being fussy about the presentation of letters and reports. It is likely that people will look at everything more carefully before letting you see what they've done. If a consultant has a reputation for being expensive but is excellent value for money, clients will expect and be prepared to pay a high fee. In a soft organization, someone who is prepared to hire and fire and stand by their decisions in order to maintain a quality service can build a reputation of being a 'hatchet man'. This perceived quality of ruthlessness can be sold to a prospective employer whose dominant culture is more macho.

Required image

The needs of certain jobs dictate the images of the people who do them. A nuclear researcher requires protective clothing, a police officer requires a readily identifiable uniform, a funeral director requires a serious and sober image. What are the image expectations within your profession or your organization and what are the image expectations of the people outside the profession – clients, customers, competitors? Not all organizations have a clearly-defined corporate image. Many do not have dress guidelines for their employees. In the absence of a formal dress code, employees can usually sense what is acceptable within the organization's culture. If it's important for you to get it right, you must look hard at the image of the successful and respected people in your profession or organization. Ask yourself whether it is a style you can emulate and whether compromises will be necessary. Will you be able to slip effortlessly into that image because it so closely mirrors your own? In the world of work it is possible, indeed very easy, to adopt a corporate persona or even several personae to match corporate expectations.

One problem I come across frequently is that of a client ill at ease in their organization because its corporate image is out of focus. If their own image is clear, they may feel frustrated and out of place. Having identified this factor they are sometimes happier making a move to a company with a strong corporate personality with which they can identify. Sometimes, people feel that they want to make dramatic changes to their image. I counsel them to take it slowly and introduce changes a step at a time. If they change overnight they cause confusion and mistrust. Their audience doesn't know which image to believe.

WHY IS THE IMAGE FACTOR IMPORTANT?

There are many routes to the top in any business. Some are based on image. Others are not. Some are ethical, some are not. Nepotism, favouritism, the casting couch, bribery and corruption and marrying the boss are all possibilities.

The ethical way is to develop an appropriate professional image and support it with an effective CV and a compelling management portfolio. The way you present yourself through the way you look can confirm or negate what you have put on paper.

There are six clear reasons why personal image is an essential device in the toolbox of career development:

- Because personal style influences the decision-makers in career development.
- Because we believe what we see.
- Because we are all busy people and we rely on first impressions.
- Because today everyone is in sales and we all have to act as ambassadors for our profession or organization.
- Because how else do you spot a star in a field of equals?
- Because looking good is good for you.

The power of personal style

One of the most significant reasons for people not advancing in their career is because of the effect of their personal style on others. The way you get things done, the way you dress, the way you behave towards

17

other people, your attitude to your colleagues and how you handle your responsibilities are all influencing factors in internal promotion and external selection.

- A financial wizard is an asset to any organization. Being unable to communicate recommendations in simple language devalues any accomplishment because everyone is bored rigid.
- Having the reputation for being sexist will spoil your promotion chances, even if your sales figures are excellent, because senior positions carry a high quotient of people management responsibilities as well as the need to meet targets.
- Being a caring and supportive manager is wasted if little attention is paid to personal hygiene and basic clothing maintenance, because people will avoid making personal contact with you.

It is a hard fact of business life that simply getting your head down and doing the job well won't get you promotion. All it will do is get you a long service award. Taking on projects that aren't part of your day-to-day duties are the ones that bring credit and recognition. Most job content is 75 per cent set duties and responsibilities and 25 per cent personal style. Stretching this percentage of personal style is the way to make your mark in the organization.

We believe what we see

In a society ruled by visual images we are inclined to believe the evidence of our eyes. If we're not sure, we can always check it out later. We are accustomed to graphics that support the written and spoken word. When the weather forecast comes on after the evening news on television, descriptions of low pressure areas or showery spells are accompanied by corresponding pictures that we can all understand. If you use a personal computer, icons replace words in a Windows programme. In politics, we look for sincerity in a politician's manner and delivery as well as listening to what they say. We are aware of any indications that the words might not match the non-verbal behaviour. 'Looking' and 'seeing' are the ways we confirm what we believe to be true. If someone looks and sounds professional we are prepared to believe that they will act professionally until or unless they let us down.

Instant information

News headlines, fax machines, phones, teletext and modems all connect us to information instantly. We're all busy people. In an ever-changing and fast-paced culture we don't have time to find out in depth or detail about every person we come across during a working day. The visual image they create is what we notice first. Their body, their posture and their dress speak before they've uttered a word. So, for practical reasons we rely on instant visual impressions when making judgements about others. We have to process the visual information as best we can, based on minimal input.

Suppose we want to ask for directions when we are travelling on the tube or passing a stranger in a lonely street. We will decide who to talk to or who to avoid, based on what they look like. This may be unfair and we do run the risk of making errors of judgement. Mistakes are made based on the only information we can collect in a short time. During the course of a working day we meet scores, if not hundreds of people, from the ticket collector at the station to the security guard at Reception; from friends, family and colleagues to strangers and mere acquaintances. If you were mentally to take a 'freeze frame' shot of yourself at any part of the day you would see what others see. How you feel, your stress level, ill or well, powerful or weak, victim or aggressor, attractive, available, approachable? Is that the instant information you intended to give out?

Everyone's in sales

Those at the top in business agree that how you dress does matter. Emphasis on customer care, quality management and empowerment means that ambassadors are needed at every level — on the shop floor, on the sales team, in the board room, at home and abroad. Going into large companies, I have noticed that the senior people — those executives with purchasing power — are usually well dressed. They see dressing correctly for business as simply another executive skill. Being well turned out themselves, they presume that someone who is inappropriately or badly dressed has other negative qualities. 'If he can't get a suit that fits — can he really impress our foreign buyers and bring in new business?' Some people don't notice these things. Others do. On a daily basis, how do you recognize the ones who notice and the ones who don't? It makes sense not to put unnecessary barriers in the way of a good business relationship by underestimating the power of personal image — whether it's with clients, colleagues, customers or competitors.

A recently-opened hotel in Japan is very keen on correct uniform. The management's view is that every member of the staff team is a walking embodiment of company culture. Wearing the uniform in the prescribed manner with immaculate grooming indicates to the customer that staff have been properly trained and will deliver the service to the appropriate standard.

Star quality

'In business you win or lose in some events every day. You need an "edge" to help you stay on the winning side.' John Harvey-Jones' remark is as true of career development as it is of business. How else do you spot a star among a field of equals, except by personal style? At an interview everyone is there because they have the right qualifications and experience but are they right for the job? Deciding whether they will fit in will depend on how they sell their personal qualities and values through their personal style. Their confidence, body language, presence and style of dressing indicate their level of star quality.

Finding a way to express individuality is important because this is the way to communicate the sought-after qualities of creativity and leadership. Whatever makes you unique should be communicated within the bounds of what is appropriate.

Looking good is good for you

Looking good sets off an upward spiral of success – a powerfully positive cycle in which the good feelings we start out with are continuously reinforced by the people around us.

Dr Joyce Brothers, Industrial Psychologist

We tend to respond most strongly to personal style and presence rather than speech, unless it is unusually interesting, forceful or decorative. We react to an individual's perception of their own competence and credibility through their image. The guts to look different and commitment to a

THE SPIRAL OF SUCCESS

Increases desire
to look good

↗

Increases
confidence

︽

Increases
performance

︽

Improves
relationships

↶

Projects a
positive self-image

↶

Increases
confidence

︽

LOOKING GOOD

Figure 1.3 *The spiral of success*

personal style are often secretly much admired. I have frequently counselled stylish dressers to stick with their style as long as it is within the guidelines of what is appropriate for their business or profession. It will not count against them unless the prejudice or ignorance of the policy makers gets in the way.

> When I started wearing what I wanted to wear my career took off.
> Sir Roy Strong, former Director of the Victoria & Albert Museum,
> writer and creative dresser

ELEMENTS OF PERSONAL IMAGE

The way you present yourself to the outside world is your personal advertisement. The way you look, your vocal patterns, your mannerisms and behaviour are all external indications of what you are able to deliver. These are separate but connected elements that register as personal image.

21

PERSONAL IMAGE

Appearance
physical characteristics
clothes
grooming

Body language
mannerisms
posture
gesture
territory
positioning

Reputation
visibility
track record
experience
qualifications

Presence
charisma
confidence
self-assurance
self-esteem

Communication style
speaking style
writing style
listening style
thinking style
presentation style

Figure 1.4 *The elements of personal image are complex and interlinked.*

Throughout your career you promise to turn up to work at certain times for a certain number of days. When you're there you promise to deliver your expertise – that's what you get paid for. Along the route to advancement you must demonstrate that you are the natural choice for whatever it is you want to do next. To do this you have to show a range of qualities that are more than the job description. Image and visibility count for nine times more than skill in terms of career advancement. All the qualities that make up a person's received image are linked, and each aspect works with the others to form a marketable whole. Individual elements are discussed in more detail in the following chapters.

EXTENDED IMAGE

We surround ourselves with the necessary tools of our trade as well as unnecessary props and accessories that contribute to our standing in the organization and contribute to our self-esteem and status. Our manners, the way we come across on the telephone and the style of our written material are extensions of our visual image. Our mode and style of travelling, the places we go to and the people we meet all contribute to visibility, reputation and professional image. We are judged on these extensions to our image whether or not we have made conscious decisions about them, or whether indeed they are in our control.

Props. The props of modern business life such as a car, laptop computer, pager, mobile phone and helicopter are heavy with the symbolism of urgency, material success and brashness. There is a need for a professional to do a stock-take on props so that each piece is used only if it is vital for them to do their job and is also an appropriate extension of their image.

Accessories. Some companies in the name of quality will issue folders, pens, diaries and so on that are part of their corporate identity. A carefully managed image can be ruined by ill-considered personal and business accessories. A general rule for watch, handbag, briefcase and pen is to choose the classic version in the best quality you can afford. Your decision will depend on your taste but should be a reflection of what you are aiming for, not where you are now.

Telephone. Your telephone image is a temporary replacement for your visual image. A clear and confident telephone style wins respect. Call for good reason, jot down the main points for the call and keep it brief. Reduce background noise and avoid talking to other people while taking the call. Taking calls when you have someone with you is rude unless it is an emergency. It doesn't make you appear important. Return incoming calls quickly and end each call positively and pleasantly, even if it's been a bit strained or heated.

Etiquette. Good manners might go unremarked but bad manners are not forgiven. Good manners can be defined as subtly seeing to the needs of

23

others while looking after yourself. A well-mannered image is created by:

- respecting your colleagues' time, space, privacy, priorities;
- observing equal opportunities policies;
- being assertive not aggressive;
- not using cigarettes, alcohol or chewing gum unless invited;
- extending common courtesies to colleagues and visitors —coffee, tea, chair to sit on, somewhere to put their coat and so on;
- avoiding gossip.

Documentation. If you don't already have one, build a reputation for well-presented documents that are clear, concise and correct. Any document that emanates from you represents you and your standards of presentation.

Travel. Keep your professional image intact when travelling. You never know who you might meet and, anyway, you get better service when you are appropriately dressed. Try to:

- book a seat whenever you can;
- travel first class whenever you can (pay the difference to ensure peace and quiet if that's what you need to get on with some work);
- buy yourself the comfort you need to function as a professional;
- plug the gap with your own funds to obtain the security and status you need.

Places. Your office, where you eat, how you travel, where you travel to, the clubs or associations you belong to are further indications of what you think you are and what your aspirations are. They influence people's perceptions of you as a professional. Your office is probably not the best place to make a strong personal statement. Asserting your preference in this way can be tricky. Conforming but adding a light touch of personal interpretation is more likely to be admired than airing personal issues through the medium of office decoration or layout.

People. Who you know, with whom you are seen, and whom you employ are all extensions of your image – like bridesmaids at a wedding, some people are employed to dress up and do little except enhance their boss's reputation. As companies get leaner so this practice will die.

> The display of sumptuosity through a third person is nothing new.
> Quentin Bell, 'On Human Finery' 1976

'Tissue rejection'

If your personal style is not in tune with that of the organization, you may suffer from 'tissue rejection'. In medical terms, this happens when the host organism spots an intruder and rejects it. It will not allow it to grow and develop because it does not share the same genetic characteristics as the host. This phenomenon can be seen in the workplace. For example, if formal business wear is the norm at work but you feel that wearing it puts you in a social or creative strait-jacket, then there is every chance you will be 'rejected'. You will have to consider the price of the compromises needed to stay there.

> As I get older I see nothing politically or morally wrong in using dress and appearance to my advantage. If I were to present myself on television in a cotton skirt and sandals I would be doing the peace movement a disservice. These days I am quite happy to dress up in a navy blue suit and my grandmother's pearls if I think it will make Tory MPs listen to what I'm saying. I guess you could call that maturity.
> Marjorie Thompson, Chair CND, interviewed 1993

Are there any exceptions?

When you are paraded because of your connections.
When you are needed because of your skills.
When you are wanted because of your knowledge.

Who can afford to ignore the rules?

The very powerful.
The very beautiful.
The very rich, who have nothing to prove.
The destitute, who have nothing to lose.

COMMUNICATION

Communication can be defined as the transfer of thoughts, ideas and feelings through speaking, listening, writing, actions, behaviour, attitude, pictures, signs and symbols. Effective communication is clear, concise and accurate. Communicating personal style should follow the same rules. Your message of competence and confidence as a professional should be clearly communicated every day of your working life. Every message needs a medium to carry it—in this case your image is the medium that carries the message of your goals and ambitions, your abilities and what you stand for. In this chapter the emphasis is on non-verbal forms of communication.

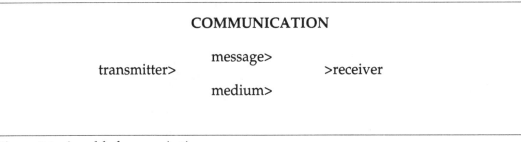

Figure 2.1 *A model of communication*

FIRST IMPRESSIONS AND THE POWER OF NON-VERBAL COMMUNICATION

First impressions count — that is why you should manage every moment of a first meeting. It really is true that you don't get a second chance to make a first impression. You might as well get it right in the first place, because it's hard work to correct an unfortunate first impression. Research shows that when people meet each other for the first time, within a few minutes 90 per cent of them will have formed a judgement that is based mainly on appearance – physical characteristics, presence, body language, clothing and grooming. This may be unfair and they run the risk of making mistakes. Any errors made are based on the only information they can collect in a short time. Ideally, we should take note of the first impressions then take the time to reflect. Common sense suggests that one should allow for a period of contemplation between the initial impression and one's acceptance of it.

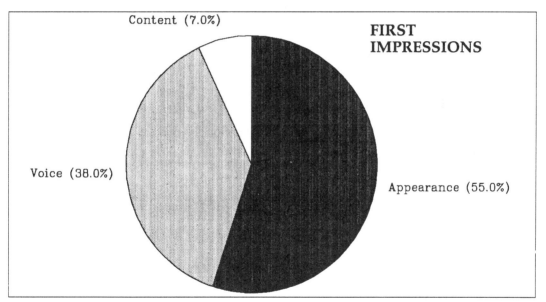

Figure 2.2 *First impressions*

Research by social psychologist Albert Mehrabian shows that 50 per cent of first impressions is based on appearance.

It is worth remembering that other people's judgements say as much about them as they do about us. Their judgements will be supported or discredited by all the 'interceptors' listed below. It is generally agreed that we notice the characteristics of another person in this order:

race;

gender;

age;

size;

facial expression, eyes and hair;

clothes;

movement and posture.

Then, in the order that is significant for us, we make judgements about their:

level of attractiveness;

personality and temperament;

level of education;

degree of success;

level of sophistication;

up-bringing;

financial status;

level of seniority;

social and moral values;

social standing.

Then make decisions about:

whether to trust them;

whether to like them;

whether to do business with them.

When we make these decisions we use a combination of 'gut feeling', observation, deduction, presumption and expectation.

Interceptors

When we get dressed we are transmitting a message through the medium of clothes to other people who are the receivers. If the receivers are on our wavelength they will pick up the signals accurately and understand the message. When the message is not received clearly or is not understood, we have to consider what is causing the interference. A variety of mental sets clutter up the lines of clear communication. I refer to these kinds of interference as 'interceptors'. Common interceptors are:

Past experience. If you usually turn up for work looking like a slob then one day when you feel particularly cheerful, want a change and put a bit of extra effort into your appearance, someone is bound to ask you if you are going for an interview. Their own past experience is that slobs only put on a good shirt and a well pressed suit when they are going for a job.

Age. The generation gap. Many older women, particularly those who are widowed, dislike the way that young women wear black from head to foot. The generation of women who went through a world war associates black with funerals or after-six wear. They prefer to see young people in something more cheerful because they see youth as optimistic. Youth in its pessimistic phase sees black as nihilistic or sophisticated or merely practical — it goes with everything and doesn't show the dirt.

Prejudice. A man who thinks women shouldn't wear trousers is blind to how attractive his wife looks in a pair of well-cut jeans.

Social factors. Underdressing at a working-class wedding could be sending out a message of sophistication but would be received as your not having made the effort like everyone else. Are the bride and groom to presume that you don't think they are important enough to dress up for? Are you indicating that you are a bit hard up, or too mean to spend money on the event?

Cultural differences. Cultural interceptors are at work when the bare limbs of foreign female tourists are regarded as a sign of availability in a country where the female form is always covered in a public place.

INTERCEPTORS

Transmitter sends out message in the form of dress >

>received as sophisticated, amusing and fashionable by those who are on the same wavelength

>received as ridiculous, disgusting, laughable and immoral****!!!!! by those who are not properly tuned in.

Interceptors at work are intolerance and ignorance.

Figure 2.3 `Interceptors' in non-verbal communication occur when transmitter and receiver are not on the same wavelength

You might like to consider how other interceptors influence effective communication: fear, jealousy, distraction, infatuation, ignorance, indifference and intolerance.

THE LANGUAGE OF CLOTHES

> Should we be silent and not speak, our raiment
> And state of bodies would bewray what life
> We have led.
>
> *Coriolanus* Act V, Scene III, William Shakespeare

Alison Lurie, the American novelist and journalist, popularized the concept of communication through dress in *The Language of Clothes* (first edition, 1982).

Articles of clothing have always had individual significance as signals of personal identity and acted as potent symbols of their time throughout the ages, from generation to generation and from culture to culture. They have the ability to speak clearly to those who have taken the trouble to learn the language. Every decade this century has an item of clothing that speaks for that decade and its social, political, economic and technological state. The short straight dresses worn by flappers of the 1920s tell of the physical and social emancipation of women. The flowers, soft lines and droopy fabrics worn by the hippies of the 1970s scream of the social trend to abhor war and return to nature. If clothes can reveal the truth, they can also tell lies. They can provide a disguise, reveal secrets or hide inadequacies. Whole outfits or even a single object can have different meanings.

Take the earring. In the 1980s the large gold earring was an obligatory accessory for a successful career woman. My mother's generation thought large gold earrings a vulgar display because small, discreet and probably pearl earrings only were worn with dressy clothes, after lunchtime. The sparkly stuff was saved for evening wear. My grandmother thought that having your ears pierced was 'common' and only for gypsies. She didn't think much of Queen Alexandra who had her ears pierced as a child, as was the Continental custom, and wore long, dangly earrings and a pearl choker, which became her personal style statement. Men who wore a single gold hoop in the time of Elizabeth I were pirates and adventurers, such as Sir Francis Drake. Today, a single gold hoop might be worn by a gay man on one ear only, clusters of hoops are worn by punks, rich young tradesmen wear them in pairs — and now they are shunned by fashionable women of the 1990s in favour of ethnic silver and beads.

A person's ability to understand the language of clothes is determined by several factors:

- the level of their clothing awareness;
- their level of interest in clothes;
- their familiarity with the range of alternative interpretations;
- their willingness to talk about clothes.

Colin McDowell robustly defends clothing as social comment in *Dressed to Kill: Sex, Power and Clothes* (1992), a densely written book that is neither social history, anthropological study nor fashion commentary but includes elements of each in the author's discursive style. He argues the case for a renewal of intelligent interest in clothing which has long been '. . . pushed aside by the majority of society'. He regrets the relegation of clothing in the form of fashion to a kind of ghetto visited only by fashion writers, eccentrics or the absurdly rich.

Whether you understand the nuances or not, body and clothes speak before you do. The conscious or unconscious visual image that is created through clothes is what we notice first. The picture that is formed by body, posture and dress speak to us before a word is uttered. We filter this visual information through our own experiences and preoccupations. When someone dresses in a style that closely mirrors our own we infer that they probably have similar attitudes, beliefs and values. We will probably be attracted to them and be more inclined to do business with them.

Character cues

There are many opportunities to transmit messages about character and style through a clever choice of clothing. When clothes are used to define character they become a 'trade mark' in the best sense of the word. I use a warm up exercise at seminars called 'Who am I?' The point of the exercise is for delegates to find out as much as possible about each other without asking any questions—to pick up any character cues they can. They have to discover the age, interests and lifestyle of their colleagues through observation and deduction rather than verbal questioning. All the information they need is available from dress and demeanour. Some find this exercise threatening. They feel that they will reveal too much about themselves through their observations—their lack of sophistication or their lack of experience at reading the signals and making sense of them, or the chance that they might embarrass someone with a tactless remark. Others are almost clairvoyant in the accuracy of their interpretation. When people introduce themselves we look at the discrepancies between their 'truth' and ours. At this stage we discover our individual levels of fluency in reading the language of clothes.

This exercise parallels people's familiarity with a foreign language. In any group one or two will need an interpreter. Their low level of understanding can spring from a sense of intellectual superiority. They are really saying, 'There is no need to understand about clothes because words and ideas are more important'. Some discover they can do little more with the language of clothes than the equivalent of ordering a cup of coffee in French. They can tell the difference between smart and scruffy, classic or avant-garde but nothing more complex. Their sheltered upbringing, conservative background or low motivation has limited their opportunities to learn the necessary vocabulary. Others find they can read the language but not speak it. They pick up accurate signals from other people but are not able to experiment 'out loud'. They have internalized and intellectualized the process and are unwilling to put it to the test in a practical way. I have also noticed a minority who wear all the right things but can't explain how they arrived at their choice. They have the ability to mimic without understanding. Yet others have a large vocabulary, lots of confidence and the guts to try new things and learn from their mistakes.

There is a difference in the way men and women respond to this exercise. Some men use the opportunity to attack or undermine a colleague. Many men feel that talking about clothes is trivial—women's talk. They are filled with paranoia when aspects of dress are discussed. Both men and women underestimate the social and political statements that clothes are capable of making. They fail to understand the link between appearance and personal identity. Fashion commentators continue to promote the notion that serious discussion about clothing should be at the centre of our interest in human behaviour. There is not yet a universal acceptance of this notion.

BODY LANGUAGE AND PRESENCE

> In Hollywood powerful people move slowly and speak slowly.
>
> Michael Caine

Communicating personal style through body language is not about projecting the right or wrong messages or giving away hidden thoughts and feelings. It is more to do with using information about gesture and mannerisms and so on to project a positive image of oneself and to be more sensitive to the non-verbal signals of others. We can all brush up our people-reading skills by looking to really see and listening to really hear. The way they move their body can show how much a person is in control of a situation, can create a strong style signature and can have naturalness or falseness. In difficult situations, nerves can inhibit natural behaviour. People ask for advice about the right way to sit at an interview. 'Should I cross my legs? Should I lean forward or sit back? What will people think if I scratch my nose?' They worry that they will somehow be caught out. Learn to sit still, breathe properly, think positively and try to behave naturally is still the best possible advice.

Professional presence

A professional demeanour will take into account the following aspects of body language:

Eyes. The ability to make and maintain eye contact looks confident; lowering the eyes appears submissive.

Face. Facial expression can show seven basic emotions: fear, anger, surprise, disgust, happiness, sadness, pain.
It's as well to know how your face registers these emotions and whether there is a chance that they might be misunderstood. Do you know

whether you have expressive features or whether your face remains a mask whatever you are feeling?

Eyebrow flash. Raising the eyebrows for a few seconds when you catch someone's eye is friendly and reassuring. Try to respond to another's eyebrow flash unless you wish to signal disapproval or hostility.

Looking down your nose. If you hold your head up and tipped slightly back when looking at someone without bringing your head forward, you appear to be looking down your nose at them and come across as aloof or superior.

Posture. The way you sit, stand and walk can make you seem confident or timid, well or ill. The stance of a soldier on parade is not necessarily good posture. To achieve a confident and upright posture, imagine a piece of string threaded through your spine, up the back of your neck and out through the top of your head. When this string is pulled gently from above it gradually lifts and straightens the chest, shoulders and head. Imagine a helium balloon tied to this piece of string that will keep your head floating above your neck.

Gesture. Gestures such as handshaking, hugging, kissing or waving are conscious actions. Others, such as ear pulling, neck scratching or paper clip destruction are done unconsciously. We use gesture to emphasize the spoken word. Gestures should draw attention to the idea or shade of meaning, and not the gesture. They are also used when listening or being passive and can be warm or cold, aggressive, submissive, decorative or entirely unnecessary. Any attempt to interpret gesture should take into account:
- the *context* in which it's viewed — crossing arms and legs and hugging oneself can indicate a high level of insecurity, on a windy station platform it indicates trying to keep warm;
- the predominant *culture* — the meaning of hand gestures can vary considerably across cultures and continents;
- what other gestures are being used at the same time — try to interpret *clusters* of gestures rather than an isolated gesture.

Territory and positioning. Our sense of personal space is very important to us. We are all aware of our invisible defensive personal zone or 'space bubble'. The comfortable distance we can put up with will vary across cultures. There are city zones and country zones. We are sensitive to the distance between people and judge their relationships accordingly. Experts agree that four zones operate in Western culture.

Four zones

Intimate zone. Six to eighteen inches (15–45 cms) from our bodies. Permission to enter this space is highly selective and a violation of this space by someone other than close friend, spouse or family can be seen as extremely hostile.

Personal zone. There are two sub-zones:
— close personal; ranging from eighteen inches to two and a half feet (45–75cms) for close friends, spouse and friendly social gatherings;
— far personal; of between two and a half and four feet (75–120cms). You can still talk to each other at this distance but the atmosphere is more formal. If you invade this space too suddenly or without an invitation it can appear either alarming or rather pushy.

Social zone. About four to twelve feet (120–360cms) across a room or piece of furniture, for example the distance between seminar leader and delegates that indicates semi-formal business, or the distance between boss and new employee to communicate difference in status.

Public zone. Anything over twelve feet (three metres). The distance firmly established when a speaker addresses a meeting. The far end of this zone is used by someone giving a speech to a group of people they don't know. It is common when a town hall employee has to address a public meeting. Unnecessary distance can lend hostility quite unintentionally. Some speakers at large meetings like to work with a roving microphone so that they can vary the zones they operate in and reach people from a less intimidating, formal and confrontational distance.

Touch

Touching at work is a sensitive issue. Warm, friendly people who instinctively touch as they talk can embarrass the cooler types. Touch can be interpreted as condescending — a pat on the head is what you give a

ZONES

public 12ft(360cms) or more

    social 4-12ft(120-360cms)

        personal   - far(75-120cms)
                           - close(45-75cms)

                      intimate 0-18" (15-45 cms)

Figure 2.4 *The acceptable distances between people in different social and personal situations*

child. Touch can be interpreted as sexual harassment—what you intended as a friendly gesture could be perceived as an uninvited sexual advance. Touch is therefore limited to the business handshake only unless there is an emergency or you want to offer support to a colleague in extreme physical or emotional crisis.

Levels of touch
Medical treatment — from a nurse or doctor to patient.
Social—professional colleagues handshake.
Friendship — hug and kiss to special friends not business acquaintants.
Love — close family only who are able to expose and respond to vulnerability.
Erotic—sexual arousal.

Business handshake. It is vital to have a good handshake, a powerful form of non-verbal introduction. Make it a clear statement of who you are, your status and intentions. Make sure you can go into your 'smile — eye-contact—handshake' routine confidently whenever it is appropriate.

BUSINESS HANDSHAKE CHECKLIST

Score: 1 = OK   2 = needs some work   3 = letting my image down

	Score
Appropriate smile	
— genuine, not too broad, not apologetic	1 2 3
Eye-contact	
— initiated and maintained for 5–10 seconds	1 2 3
Dry palm	
— not sweaty or sticky, too hot or too cold	1 2 3
Soft skin	
— not rough or calloused	1 2 3
Firm grip	
— not a cruncher or a wet fish	1 2 3
Duration	
2–5 seconds, no longer than 8–9 seconds	1 2 3
Appropriate style of grip	
— web to web, vertical, on equal terms	1 2 3
Posture — leaning slightly forward	1 2 3

Figure 2.5 *Business handshake checklist*

Women who are not used to this routine should practise it, as it is now expected that women will shake hands. They are expected to use less pressure than men.

Exercise   Try out your handshake on friends. Note what they say.

Mannerisms. Some common mannerisms can be interpreted like this:
- tilting the head sideways:
  - either shows interest in what's being said; or
  - could be a sexually submissive gesture like offering a vulnerable neck to a vampire; or
  - could be signal of giving up.
- picking imaginary fluff can indicate boredom:

      — either your mind is elsewhere; or

      — you feel disagreement that you are not voicing.

- rubbing hands together quickly usually communicates enthusiasm and energy, eagerness to get on with the job, but it can look *gauche* or over-eager;
- patting hair, checking make-up, picking at cuticles all suggest lack of confidence. The only people who have constantly to check their appearance are models because they earn their living by it.
- hands in pockets:

      — can look slovenly; or

      — powerful, depending on the accompanying posture.

BODY LANGUAGE CHECKLIST

How do I use my smile?
Do I stand up straight?
Do I make eye contact?
Do I look nervous?
How do I use my hands?
How do I walk into a room?
Is my handshake firm and business-like?
Do I stand too close or too far away from people when talking to them?
Do I touch people when I talk to them?

Positive signals	Negative signals
*using up space	*not using space
*stillness	*nervous mannerisms
*standing comfortably	*handling objects
*sitting asymmetrically	*pointing
*eye contact	*touching the face
*open palms	*clenching fists

Figure 2.6 *Personal body talk in business*

Putting your hands in jacket or trouser pocket or one hand in a side pocket as you get up to speak, and standing square to your audience feet apart, can look reassuring and business-like.

Exercise When watching TV, look at the newscaster or soap opera actors and analyze how much their facial expression supports or negates their message. Look particularly in the strong emotional or dramatic scenes.

Charisma, the gift of grace

Star quality, self-assurance, an air, an aura, charm, confidence — someone with charisma or personal presence has a mysterious appeal. Is it fixed at birth? Can you learn how to get more of it? We all know someone who walks into a room and fills it with their personality. They can command attention and when they do speak we are prepared to listen. The way they stand, the way they move and their body language communicate a strong sense of self.

REPUTATION AND VISIBILITY

Most of us are invisible. We have a small infrastructure of people who know us — our friends and family, people we meet at work, at church, at the golf club or sports centre, our neighbours and local shopkeepers — probably no more than a hundred or so people. Compared to international figures in politics, films and pop music most of us have a low level of 'well-known-ness'.

Recent research across a large number of organizations shows that there are three factors determining whether someone is promoted or not. The most influential factor is visibility or exposure. The contributing factors are made up in this way:

1. Doing the job — 10 per cent — your performance rating and how good you really are at your job and its tasks and responsibilities.
2. Image and personal style — 30 per cent — how you come across, your way of getting things done, your attitude. If these don't fit — you don't get the job.
3. Exposure and visibility — 60 per cent — who knows you, what kind of reputation you have, your contacts and published achievements.

Figure 2.7 *Reputation and visibility*

If everyone in the organization works hard, then image and visibility are more of an issue than performance.

One of the reasons why extremely able people fail to make their mark on a job or in an organization is that they give the wrong impression. They come across as being disorganized or lacking ambition, or are reticent about their interest in a high profile project. We all know able people who have been overlooked because they simply have not stated their interest in promotion. Another reason is that the contribution they are making, albeit consistently and well, is simply not on the agenda. Early in my teaching career, I ran an Arts and Fashion Department in a local adult college. I thought my role was to develop and safeguard local centres of excellence. My boss thought I was there to promote the 'bread and butter' popular courses that would subsidize the esoteric or socially worthy courses that other departments found difficult to fund. Decisions about resources were a continual mystery to me and my profile remained low as did the internal status of my department. You may have experienced decisions that seem to you to be extraordinarily wilful or illogical. If that's the case it's time to check the agenda.

Exercise

Write down what you think your job is and what you think you are actually achieving in that role. Ask your immediate boss what they think you are supposed to be doing in the job and what contribution they think you make to the department/organization. Compare notes. The discrepancy can be astounding.

Ten ways to promote yourself and increase your visibility

The workshops I run always have a session on designing self-marketing tactics and strategies. Every group comes up with good ideas. Here are some of them:

1. Be well presented

— Project an appropriate and positive professional image.
— Be consistently well-dressed and well-groomed. It has a doubly-positive effect — making you feel good as well as promoting a positive response from others.

2. Be well informed

— About the organization.
— About your role and function.
— About your specialism. Make sure you are up to date. Opinions can change, knowledge advances. Fashions in management theory can change as rapidly as street fashion.

3. Volunteer

— Volunteer to do the kind of task that brings you to people's notice in a medium to large gathering, especially if there are going to be 'influencers' present.
— Organize a seminar.
— Deliver the report-back from small group discussions.
— Chair a working party.
— Make a speech at a retirement or leaving party.

4. Get into print

— Get used to the idea of publishing what you do. This is particularly important if you have a job with relatively low visibility. You must highlight your achievements in other ways.

41

— Try a short weekly report to your immediate line-manager, The Chief Executive or Chairperson.
— Contribute to specialist journals.
— Contribute to the in-house newsletter.
— Write up a report on courses attended.
— Write to say thank you to whoever funded your attendance on a course. Tell them what you got out of it and how you will use it in your work.
— Organize tasks with your name on to be done in your absence. While you are away you are invisible.

5. Effective networking
— Learn the skills of effective networking.
— Use your contacts inside and outside the organization.
— Join appropriate associations and support groups *and go to the meetings!*

6. Business cards
— Make sure you always have a supply of business cards with you. Public sector organizations don't always provide cards so fund this yourself if necessary. 'Stickies' with your name and address on won't do.

7. Photographs
— Have a set of professional black and white photographs taken. Use them for internal or external PR, for conference programmes when you are invited to speak and to accompany articles for professional journals.

8. Make a good presentation
Speaking on platforms is the fastest route to authoritative success known to man . . . or woman. You stand there as an acknowledged authority in front of 50–100 people all of whom will remember you and the image you project.

Steve Shirley,
Interviewed 1992, in *Businesswoman*

— Check out your presentation skills. Even if presentation is your business you need to update your style now and again. Everyone can get stale or develop bad habits.
— Informal gatherings of colleagues can be a theatre for you to try out a new presentation style or newly acquired presentation skills.

— Go on a good presentation skills course. Fund it yourself if necessary.

— Present a report orally as well as write it — a well presented report or a contribution to a meeting that is intelligent, concise and interesting will get you remembered. This is particularly effective if the general standard of presentation at meetings is low.

— Learn to speak well on your feet in any circumstances.

9. Approach the recruiters

— Find out which agencies recruit in your field and introduce yourself.
— Don't put yourself up for a job just for the experience, you waste everyone's time including your own. Your lack of commitment will always show through.

10. Know the rules

In any organization there is always a system. It may be a bit cumbersome, it may be laughable, it may not even work. To get yourself noticed in the right way you have to know how the system works and learn to work inside it, straight through it or outside it altogether.

> Is climbing the corporate ladder a game? Absolutely ... If you care about your career you should take these games seriously ... If you're an employee you must figure out a way to let the true decision makers know how good you really are, without making enemies of the people in between. Keep your peers as friends ... your peers are your natural allies.
>
> M H McCormack,
> *What They Don't Teach You at Harvard Business School*

SELF-MARKETING

Can people be shaped into products? Can marketing make a success out of anyone? The answer to each question must be, 'It depends!' Some of the principles of marketing can certainly be used in the quest for visibility. Marketing is a process of examining a product in relation to a market and deciding how to maximize the product's potential. What careful and considered self-marketing can do is to help identify the best sector in which to compete and determine the best role to play.

> For the sake of your own self-esteem if nothing else you need people to know when you are doing a good job, especially those who can help you to promote yourself.
>
> Dorothy Leeds

43

> # THE MARKETING MIX
>
> * Product
> * Price
> * Place
> * Packaging
> * Perceptions
> * Promotion
> * USP — Unique Selling Point

Figure 2.8 *The marketing mix can apply to people as well as products*

In marketing terms you need to examine:

Product. Who you are, what you stand for, all your experience, skills and qualities, your management style, interpersonal style, attitude to work. Is the job really important to you or is it something you do between weekends? Are you driven? Are you a workaholic? What is your time-keeping like? Do you attend training courses or do you avoid them? Does the product (you) need any research and development? Would it be better received if you could drive, had computer skills, an MBA, could chair meetings?

Price. The price for the product is not based solely on what it is worth in salary terms. It is a negotiable package of perks, status, terms and conditions. What do you expect apart from your salary? Which elements would you be prepared to negotiate — a parking space, secretarial support, flexi-time, child care facilities? What is your bottom line? A regular review of your role, job function and job description is necessary to ascertain whether the price is right. Make sure you know what current rates of pay are for the same or similar jobs in the same or similar market sectors. Check your entitlement to pay awards, incentives, bonuses. Make sure you know about parity of pay and conditions in similar organizations. Every organization has a pay policy. Some make it more public than others. It is up to you to keep up-to-date and well informed so that you don't make a fool of yourself and ask for too much or too little.

Place. In this context, 'place' means your organization, department or section (or client if you run your own business). What is its organizational culture? Is there a written or unwritten corporate dress code — who would let you know if you had broken it? Is there a code of behaviour — getting drunk on Friday nights, not getting drunk at all? Guide-lines for when and how you can speak to the press? Consider the market sector and the type of industry you are in. What does it do/make/sell? Is it a multinational corporation? Is it a family business? Does it pride itself in being dynamic and forward-looking or does its reputation rest on tradition and old world values? Does the way you project yourself match these values? Would you prefer to work in the public or private sector? Does the job you do and the role you have show you at your best? It is likely that if you make too many compromises on a daily basis you are either in the wrong job or the right job with the wrong organization. It is necessary to monitor the environment constantly. Look for new threats and opportunities all the time.

Packaging. Advertising your best qualities means matching your image to meet corporate expectations. Does the way you look as well as your attitude and your behaviour reflect the part you play within the organization? Are you prepared to wear the 'team strip'? Does the way you come across enhance or hamper your reputation? Packaging yourself through your professional image is covered in more detail in Chapter 3.

Perceptions. How is your job perceived within the organization? What value is put on your specialism/department? A necessary evil? Glamorous but expensive? Good value for money? A good place to be promoted from? Somewhere to serve out your days? An appreciation of the perceptions about your industry and of your job will help you to understand the best ways to promote yourself.

Promotion. Every product needs a marketing campaign so that people know about it and are made aware of its features and benefits. A plan to make sure that the right people know what you can do is a sensible step in managing your visibility. Who is going to see you at work? How many of them? How influential are they? How can you influence them? Is your work project-based or people-based? Project-based people rarely have a high visibility job. Therefore they must draw attention to the work in other ways. If they are ambitious, they need to get out in front of people at a specialist conference for example, or even at a staff meeting. A team in an important but unappreciated project needs to write a report on its success and their part in its success. They could set up a presentation to demonstrate the important elements of the project to key people. A mass-marketing approach should be avoided as it leads to woolly thinking and wasted resources. The more precisely you target the market, the easier it is to design an appropriate launch plan.

Unique Selling Point (USP). Everyone has a particular combination of skill, talent, experience that makes them special. This is their unique selling point.

A word of warning

Whatever the job, being successful requires more than just doing it well. A careful marketing campaign is required to ensure you and your job get the attention they deserve. If you want to get on professionally there is usually a price to pay. You need a strategic plan to make yourself visible. You don't have to pull a series of publicity stunts but you do need to take advantage of any opportunities to highlight your work.

Be careful about the use of heavy advertising. Overt displays of attention-seeking are perceived as pushy or *gauche*. Superior results are gained by letting your achievements spread by word of mouth. Being associated with a successful project allows other people to say how good you are. It is more subtle and more effective to get to know the influencers professionally than to accost them at a social level.

At the final selection you will not make the team unless you have two key qualities: a sense of humour — the ability to laugh at yourself and to defuse a sensitive situation, and a generous nature — meanness of spirit and pocket in the name of efficiency doesn't open the right doors.

How to avoid a decline

When you've worked hard to achieve the level of visibility you want, how do you avoid becoming an unknown again? The team of authors who put together *High Visibility*—Rein, Kotler and Stoller—aimed their advice at aspiring show-biz entrepreneurs. Their seven obstacles to continued success are valid in any profession or business:

1. Uncontrollable ego —self assurance can grow into arrogance. 'The man is a legend in his own mind.'
2. Unplanned obsolescence —changes outside your control.
3. Uncoupling —leaving a partner, association, group and so losing status.
4. Age —the need to make way for youth.
5. Poor or inconsistent performance.
6. Self-destruction —you do the one thing guaranteed to topple you.
7. Scandal —whether it's true or false, scandal has the capacity to damage or destroy any career.

Mediocrity knows nothing higher than itself, but talent immediately recognises genius.

The Valley of Fear, Sir Arthur Conan Doyle

PROJECTING A PROFESSIONAL IMAGE

Always be well-dressed — even when begging.

Hindu proverb

Communication style through professional dress can be a bridge or a barrier to clients and customers. 'If they don't like the messenger, they won't get the message.' In a radio interview I heard a senior doctor advocating communication skills training for doctors. She was expressing concern at the poor image of the medical profession. It is true that the awe in which doctors used to be held is being eroded for three reasons:

1. their inability to apologize for their mistakes because of fear of litigation;

2. their bedside manner —interpersonal or communication skills, which in many cases are appalling. The high-tech environment of a modern hospital is as much to blame for this as the pressure of a GP's surgery. The result in both cases is that people are seen as a problem that needs treatment, not as people with a problem;

3. the role models of arrogant and distant consultants who are consistently rude to patients and junior staff.

Doctors as well as other professionals need the three As to communicate their professionalism and to be:

Approachable
Accountable
Accessible

If you deal with people as part of your job you need people skills just as much as your professional or technical skills. Your technical skills are taken for granted when someone consults you for the first time. What they are going to 'buy' is you.

Whatever the ingredients of a professional image there are bound to be certain constraints arising from the physical needs of the job, the day-to-day pressures and the expectations and perceptions of that job. What does a personnel manager look like? How should a senior registrar behave? When I asked a mixed group of managers to define 'professionalism' they came up with a surprisingly uniform list of essential qualities:

- properly qualified;
- well-informed;
- discreet;
- does not allow personal feelings to intrude;
- does not allow personal prejudice to intrude;
- does not criticize staff or colleagues in public;
- does not rubbish a fellow professional;
- polite;
- punctual;
- well prepared;
- self-disciplined;
- has a clear belief system;
- presents an appropriate appearance;
- does not trade on the insecurities of clients;
- does not offer professional advice they are not qualified to give;
- uses a positive approach, does not use sarcasm, or techniques that are humiliating or destructive;
- practises what they preach;
- respects confidentiality;

- respects client reluctance to participate or respond fully (because of social, cultural, financial or emotional constraints).

Exercise Read through the list and consider how these qualities apply to you in your occupation. Do you want to add anything, delete anything or argue?

PROFESSIONAL IMPACT

Your professional image is a picture that advertises what you have on offer — a 'promise of delivery'. For most professionals their professional impact boils down to five key qualities: competence, credibility, control, confidence and consistency.

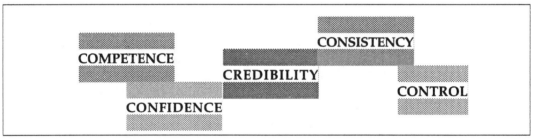

Figure 3.1 *Professional impact has five key components*

Competence

Your competence is the range of abilities that defines what you are able to do — all your skills, talents, qualifications and experience as well as the things you know you could do but haven't had the opportunity to show just yet. In this context it is useful to analyze:

What you excel at.
What you are good at.
What you can get by on.

You should be majoring, professionally speaking, on what you excel at.

Credibility

Your credibility rests on:

- Looking as though you can do the job and inspiring the belief in others that you can do what you say you can do. (I'm eternally puzzled by hairdressers with dreadful hair.)
- Sounding as though you can do the job and inspiring the belief in others that you can deliver what you say you can by using the appropriate language. Do you use the language and technical terms of your specialism correctly? Do you use it to inform rather than baffle, bore or bewilder?
- Knowing the culture and working within it. It also means knowing the rules, knowing when to abide by them and when you can break them.

Control

Self-control

Self-control is a mark of maturity. Good manners indicate self-control and are necessary all the time. Bad manners and bad temper are equated with lack of control. They show lack of respect to others. Letting your hair down or letting off steam might feel good at the time but could jeopardize the impression you want to create. Check the effect by asking afterwards, 'Was it worth it?'

Control of emotion — temper and tears

Sometimes the emotion attached to one activity, event or person spills over on to another. Frustration at a lost contract or difficult case can spill over into unnecessarily sharp words to the next person who phones. Result — temporary loss of reputation. If you give in to emotion at work you lose control and by association you lose competence and credibility. Display anger and you lose the confidence of others as well as revealing a lack of self-confidence. After a bit of a shouting match you might be advised to, 'Take a walk round and cool off.' The hidden message could be, 'Can't risk a display like that in front of our new client. Better take him off this one.' Reveal distress through tears and people will respond by remembering the tears not the situation that led to the tears. Your boss might say, 'Why not take a few days off?' while thinking, 'She's not up to the responsibility of the job — it's too much for her.' It's more profes-

51

sional to take charge and act rather than react. Managed anger in the right circumstances is effective and memorable.

Other outward signs of professional control are:

- the ability to control others which shows leadership qualities;
- the ability to control projects, being responsible about resourcing and budgets;
- the ability to be well-organized and to take control of one's own affairs by dealing efficiently with paperwork and being an effective time-manager.

Confidence

Confidence comes from the inside and shows on the outside. There are physiological signs of confidence like standing up straight and breathing easily. There are psychological ones that come from a positive mental attitude and the knowledge that you are well-informed and well-prepared.

Confidence is projected through a vocabulary that uses positive not negative terms and by not under-selling or over-selling your capabilities. Associating with positive and powerful people who value you can reinforce your belief in yourself and recharge your confidence.

Consistency

A professional demeanour cannot be put on and taken off like a coat or jacket. An image has to be consistent to be effective. Your image matters on a daily basis, not just to you but to everyone you meet. The way you look is going to influence how people respond to you, your needs and requests. A favourable impression will work for you well into the future even if it is not needed at the time, so the effort is never wasted.

IMAGE STEALERS

Thieves and robbers abound who will steal from your image and diminish your professional impact. Some robbers are the ones who visit you every day and are even invited by you. Some are encouraged by others and you might not always recognize them when you see them. Here are some you may recognize.

Competence robbers

- Self or others can make you seem less capable.
- Not acknowledging your special qualities or the effect of your input, 'It was nothing — anyone could have done it'.
- Being wrong or inaccurate when it really matters.

Credibility robbers

- Not knowing what you ought to have known, 'I haven't had time to read the report yet'.
- As soon as you insert 'but' you take away the credibility of what you say after it — '...it probably isn't very important but...'.
- 'I'm sorry' is a common vocal mannerism and used inappropriately suggests that you are guilty of something and robs you of your previous credibility. Saying sorry too often gives out messages of low self-esteem and low status. If something really was your fault, saying, 'I apologize — what can I do to put it right?' is more powerful, more credible and indicates that you are in command of the matter.
- Fluffing or flannelling in reply to tricky questions.

Control robbers

What's the pay-off of the following control robbers?

- Being late.
- Being disorganized.
- Being bad-tempered.
- Being bad-mannered.

Confidence robbers

- A small failure makes you think you are incapable.
- A criticism of a particular error or piece of behaviour downgrades your performance in your own mind, 'I knew I was no good at that anyway. I don't know why anyone asked me to do it in the first place.' 'It was only an idea, I knew it probably wouldn't work...'.

- Hesitancy in speech

Consistency robbers

- Can't be bothered today.
- No one will notice.
- Having an off-day.

Always be well dressed and well-presented. You can bet your life that the day you say, 'It's only a desk day today, I'm not meeting anyone important and anyway I have to shift all those files from the bottom of the cupboard...' it will be the day that the Managing Director of the European Division will pop in on a flying visit. It will be the one time that the TV crew appear to interview you about the research breakthrough or the leak of funds from the finance budget.

Nobody's perfect

I work from home and often work at the weekends. One Sunday morning, dressed scruffily (which I rarely am), I had a problem with the photocopier and went out to beg a favour from someone in the local parade of shops. The local estate agent was also working, and dressed scruffily.

Me, 'Are you the boss?'
Him, 'Are you the image consultant?'
Result: both professional reputations dented a little, locally.

Being wrong is human. Everyone makes errors — the trick is to learn from them. Don't keep repeating the errors, that's when they become mistakes.

Image breakers

There's no accounting for taste, they say. If you are not sure what is acceptable, consider this list of image breakers in business:

badges with slogans	visible pant line
toupées	white blouse over black bra
tee-shirts with slogans	string vest under nylon shirt
fisherman sweaters	sport shoes with a suit

running shoes	vulgar tie
leather or suede trousers	evening fabrics worn during the day
distracting hair ornaments	row of pens or pencils in top pocket
transparent fabrics	trousers heavily creased at the crutch
flowery frocks	no bra
laddered or snagged tights	no tights
bare leg visible above sock	unrelieved black

The power of grooming

Senior managers, head hunters, managing directors and other people responsible for talent spotting agree that image breakers can be grouped into dress style, clothes maintenance, personal habits and grooming. These are the most common turn-offs:

careless shave	in need of a hair cut
dandruff on collar	chipped nail varnish
overpowering fragrance	poor complexion
strange body odour	unpolished shoes
shoe heels in need of repair	bad breath

I remember a woman who came to me some years ago as part of a company executive coaching programme. She was being consistently short-listed for internal promotion, interviewed but not selected. She had prepared a good CV and had an excellent track record. The feedback from her latest interview indicated that her personal presentation wasn't quite right. I suggested she brought her prepared interview presentation to our next session and wear her 'interview outfit' for me to look at. She had made an effort but still looked a mess. She had a grasp of the rules but couldn't do it for real. Her dark grey suit and white blouse were of conventionally conservative style for a formal interview but the problem was really one of grooming. Her hair was quite short, wispy, badly cut, no shine. She wore no make up and looked grey and tired. Her hands were rough, nails short and cleanish but with ragged cuticles. She wore flesh-coloured tights that were snagged from knee to ankle and navy shoes that had never seen a coat of polish with heels permanently scuffed from driving. A worn out, large, leather-look shoulder bag overflowing with junk completed the outfit. She looked like a loser.

Her excuses for her appearance included:

- being too busy with two small children to think about herself;
- being worried that she would appear vain if she spent too much time on her appearance;
- her early childhood conditioning — her parents would have preferred a boy.

Because of her busy lifestyle she had developed bad habits in terms of safeguarding time for looking after herself. She perceived herself to be in a backstage role, rarely seen by anyone 'important'. We did some work on planning an improved lifestyle and from that she was able to raise her self-esteem. She also sharpened her perceptions about the need for a more sophisticated, well-organized, successful image. She began to understand that looking confident, well-dressed and in control would not be misinterpreted as an over-concern with self.

People don't always notice good grooming but even if they're not immaculate themselves they notice if someone else hasn't got it right. Good grooming is an important part of first impressions — every day — as well as on a special occasion. Being anxious, stressed or nervous may make you forget or skip part of a well-established routine. Some people have never developed a routine at all as a result of squalid student days or lack of parental role models. They have a hit and miss system that more or less keeps them clean, respectable and on the road. You need to design a plan that will work for you every day so that you can just forget about it. Good grooming is an important part of that vital first impression, particularly on an important occasion.

BUSINESS GROOMING STRATEGY

All over. Stating the obvious, good grooming starts with caring about being clean. There are no exceptions to the rule about starting the day with a shower, bath or wash.

Deodorant. Everyone perspires to certain degree and it's when perspiration settles on your clothes and you give them a second wearing that the bacteria combine with the air and you get an unpleasant smell. Talcum powder and an effective underarm deodorant are essentials, as is foot spray if you tend to have problem feet. Deodorant removes odour, it doesn't prevent perspiration. If you perspire heavily you will need an anti-perspirant to inhibit perspiration. It is not unhealthy to use an anti-perspirant because sweat will find another way to exit the body.

Hair. For both women and men, hair is an accessory that is worn all the time, so time and money will have to be invested to make sure it sends out appropriate messages all the time. Three vital aspects of hair at any age or stage are: cut, colour and condition. You can see to condition yourself but cut and colour should be dealt with by a professional. A good hairstyle will:

- suit your face shape and colouring;
- suit the texture and thickness of your hair;
- suit your height, body shape and age;
- be appropriate for your life-style.

If hair is long it should not be worn hanging over the face and shoulders or in a complicated style that might collapse.

Women's hair. Most women would rather go to the dentist than the hairdresser. Hair is so important to personal image and self-esteem that it pays to find the right person and put your trust in them. When your hair is cut in a strong shape it is more stylish and presents a positive image. Growing out a perm or an old style is as visually disturbing to other people as it is to you. Make an attempt to control it during the awkward stage.

Men's hair. Most heads of hair grow at a rate of half an inch every two months, so you need regular trims. If you have a bald patch, keep your hair short and avoid bringing longer hair over the bald area to try to conceal it. It has the opposite effect and always looks peculiar.

Men's face. Thorough cleansing followed by a good close shave, then something to soothe and protect the skin.

Men's facial hair. A clean-shaven look is most widely acceptable for a businessman but a beard or moustache are often worn in the more creative or academic fields. If you sport a beard you run the risk of losing credibility in the more conservative occupations such as accountancy, insurance and sales. Your beard should reflect your personality and be a part of you. A beard is not an easy option, it requires a great deal of maintenance in the form of trimming and shampooing. The surrounding facial area needs regular shaving and moisturizing as well. A moustache can be a strong style statement. It can also look silly. Try to take an objective look at yours. Hair in nose and ears: your barber should be able to clip it if you can't see to it yourself. Eyebrows that meet over the bridge of the nose look a bit Neanderthal rather than virile.

Women's face. Start with the cleanse–tone–moisturize routine even if you wear little or no make-up. Skilfully applied cosmetics with a light touch give a polish to your business image. If you use foundation, check hair line and jawline for a smooth finish and that the colour blends with your natural skin tone. Check your collar for marks. Your make-up should be in tune with your personal style. Ask yourself how appropriate it is for the outfit, the time of day and the occasion. If you are not sure how to use cosmetics effectively or feel you need an update, visit a professional make-up artist for a lesson.

Women's facial hair. An obvious moustache or a bristly chin are a bit disconcerting in a culture that does not find facial hair attractive.

Your face. Do you have a skin fitness programme? Is your complexion healthy and spot-free or does it look greying and uncared for? Business professionals, like everyone else, are exposed to the aggressive conditions of modern living which take their toll on the skin. Signs of 'added' ageing occur alongside natural ageing and are caused not only by the stress of travelling and pollution but also by exposure to sun, wind, cold and smoky atmospheres.

Shoulders. Check for dandruff, dust and loose hairs. Brush well before leaving base. Keep a clothes brush at work or in your briefcase.

Teeth. In good condition, well brushed, no traces of breakfast or lipstick. If you have neglected your teeth because of a fear of the dentist, or unhappy childhood experiences, check that this aspect of your appearance is not proving to be a multiple liability. People who are self-conscious about bad teeth rarely smile, and cover their mouth with their hands when they laugh or speak. This mannerism could be perceived as lack of confidence or shiftiness. Use sugar-free mints or a breath freshening spray after drinks or food if meeting clients or customers.

Hands and nails. Should be clean without evidence of DIY, gardening or decorating. Nails should be clean, not too long, with an unobtrusive manicure.

Fragrance. Not everyone enjoys the same smells. For an important meeting, leave it off, don't risk offending before you have even opened your mouth. If you do wear a fragrance choose a light or floral one that is not too heavy or spicy. Make sure that after-shave and perfume don't get on to your clothes. The alcohol content and the colouring could cause staining. Stale fragrance smells just that — stale.

Two reasons why professional women should wear make-up

> I like the natural look. I'd never use anything on my face except soap and water.
>
> Corporate Planning Manager

- A natural look on the face goes with a natural look in clothes. Because a casual style is rarely suitable as professional dress it has the effect of lowering the wearer's status and lessening their professional impact. Professional dressing is usually of a more formal and contrived style and therefore needs the finishing touch of discreetly applied make-up.
- We don't inhabit a 'natural' world. In our world of central heating, spicy food, air pollution and acid rain, the skin of our face is the first line of defence against the weather and the environment. Moisturizer followed by make-up provides a protective screen.

PROFESSIONAL DRESSING

Knowing how to dress well is not a gift from God. There is a set of basic skills that can be taught to anyone but they don't appear on any curriculum that I've ever seen. Psychologists agree that external image represents the inner person, and even though companies perceive personal image as integral to management style, they are slow to encourage personal development in this way. Every executive needs to project their management style through their professional image every day of their working life. Only a fool does not allow for this link between identity and appearance.

Who makes the rules?

Most people would agree that what you wear to work does matter. *But—*how do you decide what is appropriate and to whom do you listen? There is an increasing feeling that it shouldn't matter what you wear — that somehow to dictate or even suggest what you should wear is an infringement of personal liberty. Different occupations and different bosses set the tone for different kinds of work 'uniforms'. A decision about what to wear to work or for a special situation such as a presentation or an interview will be influenced by personal needs and the expectations of the 'audience'. It will be subtly influenced by social and economic trends.

It is not yet universal but the trend of dressing down for work does seem to be inescapable. Your choice will have to take into account what the dress code of the organization will support. In some organizations the dress code is written down in a staff hand book and rigidly adhered to. In others there are rules that are unwritten and unspoken and operate by example. In many companies where I have worked as a consultant, a conservatively-styled dark suit and light blouse are the only option for senior women and men. Even some progressive companies find it difficult to accept women wearing trousers to work because trousers are still connected with 'off-duty' wear and are perceived as lacking in femininity and good taste. The problem of defining good taste would occur should a company give the go ahead for women to wear trousers. Some would still come appropriately dressed for business and choose a well-cut, sober trouser suit while others would wear jeans and a tee shirt.

You have to make the decision — how do you decide what image to project? Whatever the circumstances your decision will be based on:

* the expectations of your organization;
* the prevailing culture;
* the perceptions surrounding your occupation;

- where you work, its geographical location;
- the nature of the job, what do you actually do all day, the physical aspects;
- what kind of image you need to project;
- your personal style, personality, temperament, goals and values and level of ambition.

LEVELS OF DRESS

Wearing what the organization expects you to wear shows them you have chosen to be part of the team. Choosing a wardrobe from the right level is an important first step. People often get it wrong when they move from one organizational culture to another. Moving from the finance sector into social services, for example, they may find they have pitched their look too formally for the more casual style of dress typical of a process culture that forces employees to concentrate not on *what* they do but *how* they do it. Levels of dress are graded according to the degree of formality they project. The levels of dress for women described below range from formal at level one to casual at level five. Levels one and two are appropriate for middle managers. Level three could also be worn by middle managers if the dominant culture allows. Levels four and five are not considered professional dress for most purposes and give signals of low status.

There are fewer choices for men but just as many opportunities for pitching the look at the wrong level. Level one is the only choice for the traditional occupations such as finance and the law where conservative dress is the only option, particularly if the organization is city-based rather than suburban. Men often dress at level two when really they should opt for level one. Level two is perceived as lower in status and can look flashy if not interpreted in quality fabrics using an interesting colour scheme.

Level three, although less formal, has elements of the country squire about it and therefore has a certain status if worn in the right place at the right time. It could be appropriate for a country solicitor, marketing executive, GP or teacher. Level four is the least formal and is appropriate for construction work, adventure playgrounds and rehearsals.

LEVELS OF DRESS FOR WOMEN

Level one
- Skirt suit, dark colour, matching top and bottom with conservative styling based on a man's Establishment suit, clean lines, dark classic court shoes, not much jewellery, light blouse.
- Skirt suit, dark colour, more stylish lines, contrast light colour or white blouse or shirt.
- Skirt suit, conservative style, strong* colour, clean lines.

Level two
- Skirt suit with stronger colour and more stylish cut.
- Conservatively styled dress and jacket.
- Co-ordinated or unmatched jacket and skirt, colour or neutral, texture or pattern, clean lines.
- Coat dress, conservative or fashionable cut but deeper colour or dark neutral.

Level three
- Conservative, matched trouser suit in dark colour.
- Conservative, matched City shorts suit in dark colour.

Level four
- Conservative skirt with tailored shirt or blouse.
- Conservative skirt with feminine blouse.
- Dark, tailored trousers with conservative shirt.
- Dark, tailored trousers with feminine blouse or fashion or fun shirt.

Level five
- Jumper, non-tailored skirt.
- Blouse, non-tailored skirt, cardigan.
- Blouse and shorts.
- Sleeveless, non-tailored dress.
- Sporty separates.

*Bright and deep not vivid, for example electric blue, bright Jaffa orange, strong lime green or magenta, which look out of place in a cool climate. Some strong colours look tacky when worn as a suit and are more successful worn in jacket or skirt only. Cool colours and neutrals have more authority than warms and brights.

Note: anything that should really be worn for boating, tennis, riding, aerobics, is not usually suitable for business unless the sport is your business or you own the business.

Figure 3.2 *Levels of dress for women range from ultra-formal to casual*

LEVELS OF DRESS FOR MEN

Level one

The Establishment look:
- dark suit in blue or grey, discreet pattern or pin stripe in good quality pure wool;
- cotton shirt in white, cream, light blue or discreet stripe, cut to skim the body, not too tight, collar not too exaggerated, turn-back cuffs with cufflinks;
- dark socks, no pattern, at least mid-calf length so they do not reveal flesh when wearer sits down and crosses legs;
- black shoes, brogues or Oxfords;
- discreetly patterned silk tie;
- no jewellery except for watch, cufflinks, signet or wedding ring.

Level two

The `suit, shirt and tie' look but more loosely interpreted:
- suit, fashionable looser cut, lighter neutral or a colour;
- shirt, button-down, pastel colours like pink, green, beige, lilac or stripes or checks;
- tie, strong colour or pattern, bow tie.

Level three
- Unmatched jacket and trousers.
- Navy blazer or tweed, corduroy, flannel sports coat, woollen jacket.
- Check shirt in brushed cotton.
- Denim shirt with tie.
- Shirt darker than suit or jacket.
- No tie.

Level four
- Denim shirt without tie.
- Blouson or leather jacket.
- No jacket.
- No tie.
- Jeans.
- Sweatshirt.
- Sports shirt.

Note: anything that should really be worn for boating, tennis, riding, aerobics, is not usually suitable for business unless the sport is your business or you own the business.

Figure 3.3 *Levels of dress for men have a narrower range for business*

If you really dislike the idea of 'Establishment' dressing but are obliged to conform in order to be seen as part of the team, you can break just one of the sartorial rules. Coloured socks, no tie or loud tie for men or a trouser suit, avant-garde styling or bright colours for women. (More information on developing personal style in Chapter 6.) The result will either look rebellious or eccentric or even extremely naff depending on your charisma, and confidence and the open-mindedness of your audience.

A professional can be relied upon to produce a good performance even when he doesn't feel like it. An amateur always feels like doing it but can't be relied upon to turn in a good performance.

James Agate, theatre critic

KNOW YOURSELF

Clothing is the furniture of the mind made visible.

James Laver

CLOTHES AND PERSONALITY

I look alright today — I've been 'dressed' for the telly, but usually I look as though I've scrambled up an embankment after a derailment.

Victoria Wood, interviewed 1992, in *Radio Times*

A successful dresser finds a distinctive way of dressing that is appropriate for what they do and is a true reflection of their personality. Once developed it can be adapted for any occasion. This sounds simple but is not so easy to do. Many people find it difficult even to begin to think about it.

Not everyone thinks about clothes in the same way. The way they've been brought up, their self-esteem, their self-image and their personality will all influence how they arrive at decisions when they shop for clothes and when they get dressed. Some people avoid the process altogether and wear a uniform every day. Some, especially but not exclusively men, allow themselves to be dressed by others — their wives, mothers, friends or shop assistants.

Assessing clothing personality

Even if they find it a bit difficult to think objectively about clothing, people can usually position themselves accurately on the 'Clothes-line' — an imaginary line of thinking and feeling about clothes which runs from

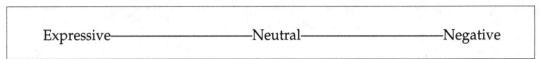

Figure 4.1 *Position yourself on the clothes-line*

Neutral out to the extremes of *Expressive* and *Negative*. Finding out where you position yourself is a useful tool to aid future decisions about business dress.

The neutral dresser has an unfocused sense of self, dresses to a 'recipe' often learnt in youth or early childhood, perhaps at boarding school, armed forces or from a protective and unimaginative mother. They can be wary of seeming vain if they pay too much attention to appearance. Though their grooming may be acceptable there is a lack of style awareness and 'street cred'. Their level of awareness of what others may deduce from their appearance is also low. They know they have to get dressed because society expects it but they neither relish nor dread the activity — it is merely routine. Their dress style is recognizable from its conformity, uninspired co-ordination and budget consciousness.

Expressive dressers enjoy clothes. They enjoy getting dressed and selecting what to wear. They always make an effort regardless of time, place or occasion and would do so whether or not they had an audience. Attention to detail is important to them and they take trouble to co-ordinate their outfits and are always well-groomed. Recognizable by their celebratory attitude to dressing, their clothes fit well and are well-maintained. They use clothes as an expression of personality and feeling. They have a positive self-image but their behaviour can tip over into obsession with clothes and appearance. Because the way they dress is an expression of individuality, the expressive would be horrified to meet someone dressed in exactly the same outfit. Expressive dressers can also use clothes as a hiding place, to act a part or as an outward manifestation of inner conflict or struggle.

Negative dressers dislike having to bother about clothes. They can look scruffy and uncoordinated. Their clothes are not well maintained, clean or pressed and do not fit well. Negativity can arise from either high or low self-esteem or a superior attitude. 'People will have to take me as I am.' Or it can come from a strong inner sense of self with no need to acknowledge external factors.

Some people make themselves deliberately unattractive out of anger. The way they look is a tangible expression of how they feel. Their anger may be at being overweight, young, disabled or different. They feel short-changed. The more unattractive they make themselves the more they suffer. The teenage girl who hides behind a curtain of long hair, wearing a long shapeless cardigan with the sleeves drooping down past her fingertips, is masking her anger and confusion about her developing maturity.

Clothes snobs

Some people set up conscious or unconscious barriers that prevent them from dressing appropriately. I meet many manifestations of the clothing personality types I have described. Some of them are snobs. They are convinced that their style and their attitude are superior to everyone else's. Clothes snobs come in many sub-types. Here are some of them:

The 'Fashion' snob. Takes an intellectually superior stance to fashion and clothing and presents a consistently dowdy appearance. They have a low understanding of the power of appearance and self-image. They see dress-sense as a superficial concern. Sometimes naive or unworldly, they make unconscious sartorial errors — running shoes with shirt and tie, court shoes with jogging bottoms, inexpertly matched colours, textures and patterns. They cannot conceive of a 'total look'. Clothes are grouped according to function not image.

The 'Personality' snob. The kind of person who thinks they have so much personal charisma that they can wear what they like. They have such confidence in their own style that they don't welcome advice from anyone, particularly image consultants. Only they know how to dress themselves because they know themselves so well. The result is that they often present an image that is slightly quaint. The Duchess of York used to fall in to this category. The 'personality' snob is fond of visual 'jokes'. They can often dress well for a special occasion like a dinner and dance or a fancy dress party. They pride themselves on knowing the right thing to wear if necessary — but the decision is dictated by them not the situation.

The 'Quality' snob. Will only wear 'good' clothes and can't understand that beauty, style, originality or flair can come from any other source. They will be well-dressed but usually just miss being stylish from fear of appearing vulgar or cheap. They are unwilling to take risks with quality for the sake of style, comfort or fashion. They are highly label-conscious and gain their security from status labels. They can be classic or fashion dressers. 'If it's a Gucci it must be OK!' Not always *nouveau riche*, typically they feel insecure about their own taste and style. A measure of their insecurity is the label worn on the outside. The quality snob tag also applies to the *nouveau pauvre* who have always dressed from Aquascutum and Burberry even if their clothes are now in shreds.

The 'Social' snob. Doesn't mind being dressed in a similar fashion to others round them, in fact they derive a certain security from this. Social dressers want to dress in the same outfit and will order (from a catalogue or a couturier depending on their status) a similar garment to a friend or colleague. Whether it be at Ascot or for a rave, peer group solidarity is demonstrated when individuals wear a similar range of garments to appear at the same social event. Social dressers are conformist dressers. They consider what other people will or might be wearing before they make their decision. When they all look the same, they are then convinced of the rightness of their decision. They fail to see why anyone would want to look different.

The 'Avant-garde' snob. This kind of dresser wears clothing in styles that have not yet reached the general consumer. As soon as the look hits the high street or preferably before then, they have moved on to something else. This kind of dresser needs an audience, preferably of the same type as themselves who will understand the nuances of their interpretations. They can be fashion victims but can also be creative and original dressers and keen watchers of trends. They mock conservatism.

Self-expression v. function

People who are unable to express themselves through the way they dress for their job feel unbearably restricted and usually opt for an unsuitable compromise. Others have developed a style that suits them off-duty but is hopelessly inappropriate for their professional life. Some people I know have managed to integrate their dress style with their lifestyle in a very successful way.

> I never have any difficulty deciding what to wear, I like clothes but don't really follow fashion. I know what suits me and have a 'costume' for every occasion.
>
> Alan Felton, actor and theatrical historian

The 'Political' dresser. Use their clothes to make a statement socially and professionally. By their own standards, they have to be the best-dressed person at any event. They don't mind being looked at — in fact their style is wasted without an audience. Their clothes can inform, entertain, amuse or provoke but they won't be ignored. They don't always understand that the expression of their view, verbally or non-verbally, is not the most important thing on the agenda.

The 'Economic' dresser. Can't bring themselves to buy any item of clothing unless it's a bargain. They haunt sales and factory shops. Spending as little as possible is more important to them than the style, colour or suitability of a garment. They often have a wardrobe full of mistakes which are actually costing them a fortune because they are never worn. They can be shrewd shoppers but often sacrifice quality for price. They may feel guilty about spending money on themselves and when they buy for themselves assuage their guilt by buying a present for someone else as well — usually the children. Women do this more often than men. They don't see that dressing cheaply will be perceived as a lack of self-esteem. Occasionally they sport a winner — more by luck than judgement — and look stunning.

The 'Body-conscious' dresser. Often well-proportioned with good body tone. This may be either by accident or design, but typically a body-conscious dresser will watch their weight, work out or play sport. They like to display what they perceive to be their assets in tight-fitting clothing, low fronts, undoing strategic buttons, pushing sleeves up to display a tan. Belts, lycra, bright colours and immaculate grooming are their hallmarks. They don't always see that too obvious a display of sexuality harms their professional image.

'Dramatic' dressers. Play a part and have a costume for everything. They are often striking looking themselves and dress to match. Whether they are playing the part of stock-broker, weekend sailor, holidaymaker, caring professional or sparkling hostess, they've got all the gear. They are amazed that not everyone wants to dress up. They can be glamorous and stylish and push the elements of their look to extremes. They don't realize that they can look over-dressed, hard or intimidating.

The 'Comfort' dresser. The first rule of clothing choice for this person is that all garments must be physically comfortable. They require clothes to fit without pinching or itching. They won't wear anything that is too tight or droopy, or that needs constant fixing. They presume that smart clothes will be uncomfortable. They often use their expressed need for comfort to disguise laziness or not being able to cope with a more sophisticated style of dress and look about as elegant as a bag of groceries.

COLOUR AND PERSONALITY

Using colour in the business wardrobe is not just about aesthetics and appropriateness. Colour preference has a psychological element which can reveal a sense of identity and how comfortable a person feels with

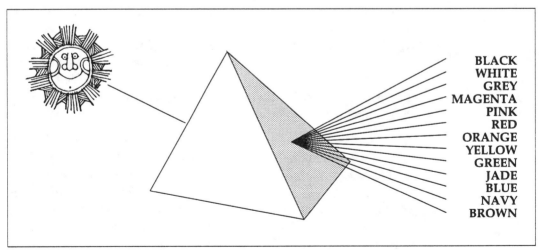

Figure 4.2 *Colour preference can act as a clue to personality*

themselves. I use a simple colour preference test as a warm up in some sessions. It is surprisingly accurate. I work with a small family of neutrals (blacks, whites, greys, browns and navies) and colours (pinks, reds, oranges, yellows, greens, blues and purples) and ask people to choose their favourite and least favourite colour. This exercise also helps to establish whether the dominant colour they are wearing truly represents their personality. I notice that some people choose colours that are technically opposites (complementary opposites like yellow and purple) which represent opposing characteristics. The colour they like represents what they see as their good qualities and the colour they don't like stands for the qualities they don't like in themselves or others. Other people choose psychological opposites (magenta and brown) indicating two sides to their own nature, one aspect of which they do not like or admire at the moment. Several dynamic women have selected magenta which reflects their outgoing, glamorous side and brown which reveals the home-maker. Both qualities can exist to a greater or lesser degree of comfort in the same person.

Below is the list of colours that I use with three aspects of their application: colour associations — symbolic, psychological or other association; personality indications — what choice of colour reveals about someone's personality or current frame of mind and appropriateness — the colour's suitability for use in a professional wardrobe.

Black

- *Associations*: dramatic, elegant, death and mourning, heavy, old, solid.
- *Personality indications*: sophisticated, lazy, everyone else wears it, doesn't show the dirt, going through a time of indecision, choices to be made.
- *Suitability for professional dressing*: not head to foot but fine as top, middle or bottom garments or as accessories. A daunting colour if you work with children or the elderly. Black shows up ironing marks, dust, fluff and cat's hair.

71

White (including soft whites, ivory and cream)

- *Associations*: cleanliness, purity, hospitals, hygiene, sterility, winter, peace.
- *Personality indications*: can be neutral, a non-communicator, over-fussy, concerned with order and cleanliness.
- *Suitability for professional dressing*: good for shirts and blouses, not suitable head to foot, not accessories. Could use for high impact image at a conference or sales presentation. Avoid if you don't enjoy spending time, effort or money on grooming and laundering as it shows every mark.

Grey

- *Associations*: neutral, ethereal, artistic, respectability, modesty, old age.
- *Personality indications*: reliable, balanced, conservative, unwilling to make commitments, unwilling to make themselves visible.
- *Suitability for professional dressing*: excellent through all tones, but needs a small injection of colour to make it interesting. Not suitable for accessories except as a fashion statement by a woman. Less authoritarian than black and dark navy. Suitable when negotiating a contract or dispute. Good for interviews when worn with white or a flattering colour. Grey does not make an impact in the creative arena unless the cut is non-traditional.

Magenta

- *Associations*: considered to be an 'artificial' colour, feminine, glamorous (sometimes called 'tart's' pink!).
- *Personality indications*: rather a dramatic personal style, likes company, likes an audience, can be a bit self-centred, is confident and self-assured.
- *Suitability for professional dressing*: not top to toe, not for men, not for leather accessories, good for silk. In its softer forms acceptable as men's ties. Is rather unpopular as a presentation colour, projects hard, tough, brittle, lack of sensitivity. Can look elegant on a woman for formal, outdoor events.

Soft pinks (including raspberry, coral, candy floss and peach)

- *Associations*: the colour for girl babies, candy floss, roses.
- *Personality indications*: approachable, feminine, sentimental — could be a soft touch.
- *Suitability for professional dressing*: use sparingly to soften harder, darker and neutral colours. Not for leather accessories. Baby pinks do not indicate management material. Good for shirts in the lighter tints.

Red

- *Associations*: the colour of hearts and flames, stands for power and sexuality, hot, dangerous, passionate.
- *Personality indications*: passionate, needs to be right, a leader, can be aggressive, a bit overbearing, is willing to take risks, sign of emotional strength, confident, exciting.
- *Suitability for professional dressing*: not head to foot, not for leather accessories. Good for woman's jacket, blouse or scarf, or man's tie. Right for occasions when you need to be recognized. Wrong for when you are tired or depressed and not able to live up to it.

Orange (including tangerine, peach and pumpkin)

- *Associations*: warm, Jaffa oranges, energy, hospitality.
- *Personality indications*: likes to have fun, is a sociable type, not always very self-disciplined, a bit common, flighty.
- *Suitability for professional dressing*: only in small quantities. The least professional colour, it can look cheap and immediately downgrades status.

Yellow

- *Associations*: the colour of sunshine, daffodils, bananas, cowardice and deceit.
- *Personality indications*: rather disorganized, outgoing, has creative thoughts, sense of humour, impulsive, is willing to experiment. Cheerful, optimistic, lively, happy, a bit juvenile at times.
- *Suitability for professional dressing*: only in small quantities,

women's jacket if cut is conservative. Yellow has frivolous conno-
tations so is not good for serious business meetings. Yellow/black
combination worn by nature's aggressors.

Greens (including grass green, olive, moss, pine)

- *Associations*: tranquil and pastoral, fresh, the colour of trees and
  grass, associated with fertility and magic but is also the colour of
  mildew, poison and jealousy.
- *Personality indications*: a nurturer, prefers informality, helpful, a bit
  shy, kind, tends to laziness, boring, predictable.
- *Suitability for professional dressing*: only in small quantities,
  women's jacket if cut is conservative, men's tie as part of a pattern.
  The deeper greens are acceptable business wear for women but not
  for men unless dressing down, or more fashionable dress is the norm.

Blue green

- *Associations*: the sea, tranquillity, repose, informality.
- *Personality indications*: perfectionist, polite, likes tidiness but not
  necessarily order, likes family traditions and special occasions.
- *Suitability for professional dressing*: only in small quantities,
  women's jacket if cut is conservative, men's tie as part of a pattern.
  Introduces a note of casualness or informality to darker colours.
  Popular colour. Doesn't offend people.

Blue

- *Associations*: the colour of the sky and sea, space, calm, depression,
  the most popular and the most worn colour in the Western world.
  Medium blues look good on TV. Light blue looks young and sporty.
- *Personality indications*: calm, friendly, conservative. Slow to trust
  but loyal when trust is deserved.
- *Suitability for professional dressing*: light blue in the summer and
  for shirts and blouses, medium blue for ties, jackets, skirts and trousers. Only the darkest shades suitable for suits. Blue and creativity
  and originality don't go together so won't be right for PR, design or
  marketing if pitching an alternative approach or solution.

Navy

- *Associations*: royal, deep and navy blues have associations with esteem, dignity and wealth.
- *Personality indications*: organized, conservative, logical, neutral. Prefers classic looks and objects. May not respond eagerly to new ideas or new methods.
- *Suitability for professional dressing*: Excellent, but needs a touch of colour to keep it interesting. Doesn't promote success and confidence to strangers unless worn in classic Establishment style and in good quality.

Purple and lavender (from periwinkle to plum)

- *Associations*: a strong violet is not often found in nature and so is considered an artificial, sometimes vulgar, colour. Purple is dramatic and sophisticated and associated with royalty and dignity, lavender and lilac with Oscar Wilde and poetry and sensitivity.
- *Personality indications*: artistic, sensitive, intuitive, slow, daydreamer, good listener, spiritual, impractical.
- *Suitability for professional dressing*: mid-tone and deep purples are alternatives for women who don't have to wear conservative navies and greys. An alternative to black for glamour. Not suitable for men except in small quantities. Dark and light tones can be very effective mixed in the form of a pattern for a tie or worn as braces.

Brown (including chocolate, golden and earthy tones)

- *Associations*: rich and fertile like the earth or sad and wistful like damp autumn leaves. Associations with piety as in a monk's habit.
- *Personality indications*: close to the earth, dislikes pretensions, solid, natural, needs to look after people, unsophisticated, homely.
- *Suitability for professional dressing*: the darker, blacker browns work as an alternative to the more conservative greys and navies for men and women. Good for leather accessories. The richer, warmer browns are unthreatening and will help people to open up to you. At public functions you are likely to disappear into the woodwork.

Selecting colours for business dressing

Selecting appropriate colours for business dress will depend on:

- The need to send symbolic messages
  — chairing a trade union meeting, will you need your red tie to show your socialist affiliations?
- Utility
  — are you a natural attractor of dirt? If you are, your choice will be governed by the need for darker more practical colours so that you look the part and are not let down by maintenance problems.
- Personal style
  — colour has the ability to convey strong messages about personal style. We need to have colours that will help us to blend in, as well as to make us memorable.
- Expectations
  — the colours that are expected in your role and at your level. You may be limited by convention to light and dark neutrals or your status may allow you to use opportunities to be more creative with colour.
- Mood
  — we start the day by being guided by our intuition. The colours we choose can enhance or underplay current mood. If you feel positive and full of beans, wearing red or yellow could exhaust everyone round you by the end of the day. If you are feeling fed up, opt for the more cheerful colours to give you a spiritual lift.

DESIGN AND PERSONALITY

Do you consider yourself to be well dressed for work? If you do, you will probably be wearing clothes that obey a certain set of rules. Whatever the occasion you will have selected an outfit that:

- suits your personality;
- feels comfortable;
- is fit for the purpose;
- is aesthetically pleasing — following the rules of good design.

The basic components of design include colour, line, shape, detail, pattern and texture. These are the tools used to implement the principles of balance, proportion, harmony, emphasis and contrast. This simple set of rules will help you to co-ordinate your business wardrobe.

Rules of basic design

Simple Rule 1

Choose a maximum of three colours for the main pieces of your outfit. Neutral gives a professional look.

Colour
- Cool, dark and muted colours recede and make forms appear smaller, which is why they are thought of as 'slimming' colours.
- Warm, light and bright colours advance and make forms appear larger and more noticeable.

Simple Rule 2

Select clothing and accessories that have uncluttered, clean lines and simple shapes for a strong professional impact.

Line and shape
- Lines can be curved or straight.
- A clothing line describes the silhouette of the garment.
- The structural line, the line created by construction seams, goes from front to back and side to side, and includes hems, pleats, and set-in sleeves, and the fall of cloth in a draped neck-line.
- Decorative lines usually have no construction function although they could follow a construction line as in three row top-stitching on shirts, or rows of braid round a skirt hem.

Simple Rule 3

Use detail as a focal point, not all over, unless your personal style is strongly decorative.

Detail
- In construction: rouleau loops as buttonholes, belt loops and tabs on trousers, smocking, shirring, double cuffs.
- As decoration: leather trim on pockets, shells for buttons, fringing, studs, eyelets, piped insets, epaulettes, ribbon ties.

Pattern	• All-over patterns, woven or printed on to the cloth, fall into five groups: stripes, checks, spots, florals, abstracts. • Areas isolated for decoration, for example a printed logo on front of tee-shirt.

Simple Rule 4

Avoid mixing patterns in a single outfit, it requires a very good eye to get it right. If you do mix, then make use of scale such as a tie with tiny dots worn with shirt of medium stripes.

Texture	• Nylon, glazed cotton, satin, lamé, taffeta and silk are cool, reflecting light and creating a smooth, shiny surface. • Flannel, felt, corduroy, tweed, Viyella and angora are warm, absorbing light to create a dull, matte finish.

Simple Rule 5

Consciously combine textures to create interest either by contrast or blend, for example a woollen (teddy bear type) fabric jacket worn with flannel trousers, moleskin waistcoat and a needlecord cotton shirt with knitted tie and leather shoes accessories projects a blended, soft look.

Some elementary principles

Balance	• Use colour, shape and texture to balance the body's natural silhouette. • Clothes appear well balanced and hang best when they fall from a well defined shoulder-line. For example you can balance a rounded or narrow shoulder line with padding or design detail. Balance a wide top half and narrow lower half with smooth gabardine on top and textured tweed below.

Simple Rule 6

Colours have a natural visual weight so use the darkest tones at the base of your outfit, for example wear black shoes with a grey skirt and white blouse.

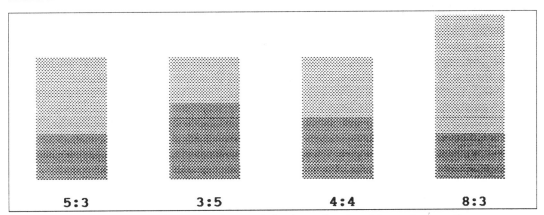

Figure 4.3 *Proportion is an important element in business dressing. Unequal proportions are more dynamic visually*

Proportion

- The relation of the size of the parts to the whole and each other, every item in scale and proportion to every other item and the wearer.
- The sculptures and buildings of the Greeks were based on proportions sometimes referred to as the Golden Mean which are in the ratio of 3:5, 5:8, 8:13: in a classic suit, the jacket proportion should represent 3 (or 5) the skirt 5 (or 8) and the jacket and skirt combined 8 (or 13).

Simple Rule 7

Remember the 'Golden Mean' — 3:5:8. Equal divisions create a low level of visual interest. These proportions don't have to be measurably accurate, but observable.

Harmony

- Suggests the sharing of common features through colour, line, shape, texture.
- Combining the parts into a pleasing or orderly whole so that it is satisfying to the eye.

Simple Rule 8

Select garments for an outfit making sure that each one connects with others through a conscious design theme, not because it was the next one clean!

Contrast

Contrast using texture: silk blouse worn with rough tweed jacket and gabardine skirt accessorized with pearls (shine) and suede shoes (matte).

Contrast using colour:

suit	shirt	tie
charcoal grey	icy pink	raspberry/black/grey
deep navy	soft yellow	mustard/navy
jacket	**blouse**	**skirt**
tan	cream	rust/brown/cream
pine green	magenta	black

Simple Rule 9

Select high contrast to project authority, warm blends for approachability or cool blends for sophistication.

Simple Rule 10

Everything you wear or carry or use should be marked by your style signature (see Chapter 6). Use the checklist opposite to see how effectively you are using the element of detail to design your image.

These guide-lines should support your everyday decisions about what to wear. They won't give you a good eye if you weren't blessed with one, but could well stop you from making some howlers.

> I usually look like a bag of shopping.
>
> Libby Purves, radio presenter and journalist

Emphasis

- Don't underestimate the power of props and accessories. Use them to emphasize attractive features and to draw attention away from others. Embroidered cuffs or cufflinks emphasize elegant hand gestures.

ACCESSORIES

	I have	I need to buy	Style signature
Hats	☐	☐	☐
Scarves	☐	☐	☐
Spectacles	☐	☐	☐
Sunglasses	☐	☐	☐
Earrings	☐	☐	☐
Necklace	☐	☐	☐
Brooch	☐	☐	☐
Belt	☐	☐	☐
Buttons	☐	☐	☐
Belt buckles	☐	☐	☐
Braces	☐	☐	☐
Watch	☐	☐	☐
Handbag	☐	☐	☐
Briefcase	☐	☐	☐
Wallet	☐	☐	☐
Purse	☐	☐	☐
Tights	☐	☐	☐
Handkerchief	☐	☐	☐
Powder compact	☐	☐	☐
Socks	☐	☐	☐
Shoes	☐	☐	☐
Gloves	☐	☐	☐
Umbrella	☐	☐	☐
Diary	☐	☐	☐
Pen	☐	☐	☐
Pillbox	☐	☐	☐

Figure 4.4 *Props and accessories checklist*

CHAPTER 5

ORGANIZATION AND PLANNING

O Wad some Pow'r the giftie gi'e us
To see oursels as others see us!
It would frae mony a blunder free us
And foolish notion:
What airs in dress and gait wad lea'e us
And ev'n devotion

To a louse - on seeing one on a Lady's Bonnet at Church
by Robert Burns 1759–96

AGGRESSIVE OBSERVATION

Aggressive observation is the technique of looking to really see and attempting to see yourself as others see you. I use this technique in workshops and seminars to help people tune in to themselves visually. They learn to look without listening so that they can concentrate on the visual messages. Look in the mirror and assess what you see without being judgemental. Avoid the trap of letting self-deception or emotional baggage mist over what is really there. This is not meant to cause a blip in your self-esteem but to stop you either dwelling on the negatives (typically a female response) or being unrealistically positive (the usual male response).

Exercise

The first stage of this exercise is like having a scan in hospital. Dress as you would for an ordinary working day. Scan slowly from top to toe, side to side, back and front and just see what's there. Attempt to be dispassionate, as though you were looking at a stranger. The second stage is to make an objective assessment about the assets and liabilities of your appearance — physical characteristics, clothes and grooming. Decide which aspects are positively working for your professional image, project your personality and accurately reflect your personal standards, goals and objectives. Then consider honestly which aspects are liabilities and could be forming a barrier to your success.

Image scan

Smile. A genuine smile at the appropriate time and place is a great asset; it's friendly, disarming, confident.

Sparkle in the eyes. Does it show a sense of humour, energy and enthusiasm?

Facial expression. Some people have the kind of face that goes sour or cross-looking or tired when in repose. A frown appears, the mouth moves down and the chin juts out a bit. This look doesn't necessarily mean you are depressed or angry, you just look as though you are. Do people always make comments about your expression and say things like, 'Cheer up', 'What's wrong with you?' If this happens to you, ask for a second opinion. Some people say these things and don't mean them, it's just an irritating mannerism. If you've got one of those faces, however, try raising your eyebrows and widening your eyes occasionally at meetings or during an interview. This will release the frown and bring the corners of the mouth up.

Posture. Do you stand straight and give an air of self-assurance and confidence, or do you stoop or cross your legs and cross your arms in an over-protective manner? Do you think you come across as aggressive, domineering, weak or submissive? Ask someone for a second opinion.

Fitness. Do you look fit and well or a bit tired and stressed? By looking as though you have energy and take care of yourself physically, people will presume you will be able to manage other things just as well. If you are not fit and well — why not? Can you do anything about it? If you can't then you can dress well, have immaculate grooming, think, speak and act positively and shift the focus away from your illness or disability.

Weight. If you are under-weight or over-weight for your height and build and feel self-conscious about it, are you compensating by dressing, standing or sitting in a way that projects your perceived liabilities instead of your assets?

Height. Do you think you are too tall or too small? Check that you are not over-compensating. A woman of five foot two in very high heels simply looks as though she's trying too hard. A man over six foot who stoops is unconsciously apologizing for his height and loses status.

Glasses. Do they fit, do they suit you, are they polished, are they up-to-date? Old-fashioned glasses are very ageing. If you wear glasses, check you keep them with you! Avoid fussy strings and chains round your neck.

Clothes-fit. An elegantly loose fit is appropriate whatever the styling. Check that all major garments fit your particular build. Trousers, jackets, coats, skirts and sleeves should all be the right length for you — not too long or too short, too tight or too loose. The fit should also reflect the right cut for you, one that reflects the angles or curves, the proportion and balance of your body. A jacket can fit by measurement but be wrong in cut — designed for someone taller or with wider shoulders or shorter waist. If you always have trouble finding clothes to fit even though you are a standard size, try other manufacturers because the problem could be the cut not the fit.

Jackets should sit well across the back, shoulder and bust/chest. Pockets and pleats should not pull or gape open. A triple mirror helps you to see all angles. Shirt collars should not be too tight — loose enough so that you can put a finger comfortably between collar and neck but not so snug that your flesh bulges over it. The shirt body should be cut loose enough to avoid over-creasing and so that the buttons and buttonholes don't gape at the front.

Trousers and skirts should have a comfortable waist band that doesn't roll over and is not too tight, especially over stomach and hips where most creasing occurs. A straight skirt should have just enough ease for you to twist it round the body. Trousers should have enough ease at crutch, seat and thigh to prevent creasing and shine.

Clothes-quality. It is not always easy to recognize quality by the price tag as some expensive clothes are rubbish and some cheaper clothes are excellent value for money. Natural fibres such as wool, silk, cotton and linen look better and last longer. So do fabrics that contain a large percentage of natural fibres. Some fabrics from the polyester and viscose families can go dull and limp. Washing and constant wearing causes the surface texture to suffer from pilling (forming tiny balls). But there are now high quality synthetics available, especially in women's wear, with the properties you would expect from natural fibres.

Clothes-care and maintenance. A maintenance checklist should cover whether all items are clean, pressed or steamed, checked for stains, checked for perspiration, with no missing buttons, loose hems, unravelling buttonholes or hanging threads.

Clothes-age. Be honest about whether any of your clothes are either worn out or out of fashion.

Being screamingly up to date is not necessary or appropriate for a professional image. However, fashion is a reflection of what is happening in society as seen through the eyes of designers. Being in touch with what is current is vital. If you've lost touch with current fashion, people will presume that your thinking and your ideas are a bit *passé* as well. Go with fashion as far as you can while still reflecting your own taste and style, the needs of your age, your colouring and figure type, the needs of your lifestyle and your professional image.

Shoes. There are still people about who judge character by shoes. A professional image means being particular about keeping your shoes clean, well polished or brushed, comfortable but smart and well-fitting. Too loose and they look like barges and slip off the back of your heels as you walk, or make an irritating clacking noise — a real turn off to others. Too tight and they go out of shape and spoil your posture and your image and will also ruin your feet. Keep all your shoes in good repair, heels not scuffed or worn down. Rotate your shoe wearing so that each pair can rest and recover between outings.

Accessories. Consider their age, style, quality and suitability. Are your accessories in keeping with your total look? A classic style of dress needs good quality, classic accessories unless you are making an alternative style statement.

Jewellery. Whether it's the real thing, costume jewellery or a piece from a designer/maker it should be good of its kind and contribute to your style statement. Sentimental jewellery such as name bracelets, fine gold chains and 'love' necklaces are too personal. They don't make a strong enough style statement and add unnecessary clutter to a business look.

Underwear. Working from the inside out check that your underwear gives you an appropriate line under your clothes. Check for anything showing that shouldn't be showing. Visible underwear, except as a strong fashion statement, is not part of a professional image unless your business is to promote underwear or sell sex. The visible pant line (VPL) under skirts or trousers is not acceptable. Always check your back view.

Grooming. People who are successful and well-groomed themselves find it hard to see past poor personal presentation. Be ruthless about observing your own grooming and assess whether it is an acceptable level for the image you need to project.

THE ASSETS AND LIABILITIES OF YOUR IMAGE AS YOU SEE THEM

Scoring system:
1. A real asset
2. Needs some work on it
3. Neither for nor against your image
4. Making it difficult
5. A liability

physical characteristics

– smile	1	2	3	4	5
– sparkle in eyes	1	2	3	4	5
– expression	1	2	3	4	5
– posture	1	2	3	4	5
– fitness	1	2	3	4	5
– weight	1	2	3	4	5
– height	1	2	3	4	5

clothes

– fit	1	2	3	4	5
– cut	1	2	3	4	5
– quality	1	2	3	4	5
– maintenance	1	2	3	4	5
– age	1	2	3	4	5
– colour scheme	1	2	3	4	5
– style	1	2	3	4	5
– comfort	1	2	3	4	5
– appropriateness	1	2	3	4	5

accessories

– shoes	1	2	3	4	5
– glasses	1	2	3	4	5
– bag	1	2	3	4	5
– briefcase	1	2	3	4	5
– jewellery	1	2	3	4	5
– underwear	1	2	3	4	5

grooming

– skin	1	2	3	4	5
– face	1	2	3	4	5
– cosmetics	1	2	3	4	5
– shoulders	1	2	3	4	5
– teeth	1	2	3	4	5
– hands and nails	1	2	3	4	5
– hair	1	2	3	4	5
– fragrance	1	2	3	4	5

Figure 5.1 *Image audit*

Make a promise to do something about the low scoring items.

PERSONAL ARCHITECTURE

YOUR PHYSICAL CHARACTERISTICS	
* Colouring	
* Silhouette	– height
*	– weight
*	– scale
*	– balance and proportion
*	– body-line – angles and curves, silhouette
* Posture	
* Fitness and health	

Figure 5.2 *Personal architecture*

Colour

This section deals with colour and its relationship to the business wardrobe. Ideally, you look for colours for your clothes that are a reflection of your own colouring so that you achieve a natural harmony. It's not just the colour (hue) that's important, it's also depth, clarity and undertone.

DEPTH	deep
	medium
	light
	bright
CLARITY	medium
	muted
	warm
UNDERTONE	neutral
	cool

Depth is the easiest aspect of a colour to see. All colours have their light, medium and deep tones. Some colours in their pure state are naturally lighter than others. Yellows and oranges at the top end of the spectrum are lighter than the blues and purples at the bottom end. Colours are made darker when black is added to them:

blue + black = navy
red + black = burgundy
yellow + black = chartreuse, the darkest form of yellow that is recognizably yellow

Colours are made lighter when white is added to them.

red + white = pink
yellow + white = ivory, the lightest form of yellow that is recognizably yellow

Clarity describes how pure a colour is. Every colour has its clear, clean version — a true colour without black or white added. Every colour also has its soft, muted or sludgey version which starts as a pure colour with the addition of black, white or grey or another colour.

grey + white + a small amount of blue = pearl grey
grey + black + a small amount of red = rose brown

Some people find it difficult to distinguish a colour's *undertone*— whether it has a blue (cool) or yellow (warm) base. Imagine red in the centre and move out to the left to find warm colours and to the right for cool colours. When you join the blue and green to make a circle you can make a warm blue with a touch of red and a cool green with a touch of yellow.

COOL   **WARM**

green<yellow<orange<orange red<**red**>magenta>blue red>violet>blue

Figure 5.3 *Undertones of colour*

Colour analysis

Some people have a good eye and can create interesting colour schemes that complement their own colouring. Even people with a good eye can find it difficult to assess their own colouring characteristics. If you are not sure about what suits you, arrange to see an image consultant who has been trained to assess personal colouring. Having an image consultation is not a luxury or a vanity these days. It is a necessary part of building a professional image. A good consultant can establish your unique colour profile by analyzing your hair colour, eye colour and skin-tone. A palette of colours will be selected for you that will harmonize with your colouring and co-ordinate with each other.

Colour schemes

What sort of colouring do you have? Here are some examples of using your own colouring as a starting point for a co-ordinating colour scheme:

- dark hair + dark skin tone + dark eyes = wear dark + dark blend.
  For example — brown jacket over a black dress or cream (a deep shade of white) shirt and brown trousers.
- light hair + light eyes = wear light + light blend.
  For example — stone jacket with white blouse or grey suit and icy pink shirt.
- dark hair + lighter skin + bright eyes = wear dark + light (go for contrast — the darker the hair and paler the skin, the more contrast you can have in your colour scheme).
  For example — black jacket and white shirt or deep or charcoal suit with sky blue shirt or navy blazer worn with stone trousers, or
- dark hair + lighter skin + bright eyes = wear dark + bright.
  For example — red jacket over a deep pine green dress.

To be on the careful side, you can always opt for the safe medium tones that do not have a dominant characteristic, for example:

- medium navy suit + soft white shirt + turquoise and jade tie;
- coral blouse + flannel grey jacket + darker grey skirt.

Clothes are usually chosen first by colour then by style or function. People are instinctively drawn towards a particular colour or family of colours which may or may not suit them. Sometimes colours are chosen that are a closer match psychologically than physically and their choice is an expression of temperament and personality rather than aesthetics. An outgoing and sociable person might choose an orange-red in tune with their capabilities as a leader and positive thinker which clashes with their muted colouring. Sheer force of personality often overcomes these apparent mismatches. If you choose a small family of colours for your clothes and limit prints and patterns you are more likely to have clothes that can be worn with each other.

Colour preference

I have found that people are instinctively drawn to either (a) specific colours, 'I only wear red... or beige... or green... ' and are narrow-minded about the rest of the spectrum, not considering neutrals to be colours, just wearing them as a basic backdrop, or (b) one of these four broad colour groupings:

Neutrals. Blacks, whites, greys, beiges, pebbles on a beach, porridge and string.
Naturals. Browns and greens of leaves and trees, earthy, terracotta, rust, herbs and spices.
Colours. True clear colours, primaries and secondaries, colours of the rainbow.
Neutrals with colours. For example navy, white and red, anthracite, pearl and jade, camel, cream and peach.

All these colour groups have a natural harmony but may not necessarily flatter the wearer.

Complementary colours

One way of looking for a flattering colour to wear is to establish your eye colour and then look for its complementary opposite. If you choose to wear this colour close to your face it will usually enhance your eye colour and flatter your face. Why not try it and see? Men could use this idea for a new tie colour, women for a flattering blouse or scarf worn close to face.
Here are some examples:

Eye colour	Complementary opposite
clear bright blue	yellow/orange
blue-grey	coral, soft fuchsia
blue-green	warm, bright pink
hazel	true blue, purple blue

green	true red
aqua	coral
light brown	turquoise, soft navy
deep brown	pine green, forest green

The secret of a successful colour scheme is to select colours that you *like*, that like *you*.

Primary physical characteristic

In order to determine how to dress appropriately to enhance your build, weight and height you need to decide which of your physical characteristics is the most obvious. Then make sure you dress it to advantage. There are five elements to this exercise which can be done by observation or measurement. You need to establish in a fairly general way your primary physical characteristic:

Height: tall, medium or short.
Weight: overweight, underweight, average.
Scale: large, medium or small.
Balance: top heavy, bottom heavy, evenly balanced.
Shape or line: curves and contours, straight lines and angles, a mix of both.

Common sense and objective observation are the key skills needed for this exercise. You need to look at the total picture you present and avoid the two most common dangers — zooming in for a close-up on real or imagined defects and hyping your assets. Decide what it is that people see first when they look at you, then dress that element to its most flattering extent.

LIFESTYLE

What do you spend most of a typical week or month doing? Do you go sailing at the weekends? Spend as much time as you can with the family? Take work home? Are you decorating or renovating a house? If you are in full-time work you will spend on average 10–12 hours a day working and travelling, 2–3 hours eating and preparing food and household chores, 2–4 hours at leisure and 8 hours sleeping. Some people keep the same clothes on all day and just roll on from one activity to another: staff meeting, cooking chips, personal computer, watching TV, taking the dog for a walk, then all the clothes come off at bed-time and a fresh lot worn the next day.

Other people have an outfit for every activity. Work clothes are stripped off as soon as they get in and they put on track suit or tee-shirt and leggings or their special dog-walking clothes. Sometimes the strip is a symbolic gesture to separate on-duty from off-duty and sometimes for practical reasons to keep work clothes clean and in good condition and not spoiled by lounging about, dealing with small children, animals or household chores.

Whatever your life style you can't support it unless you work. This means that time, effort and money have to be invested in maintaining your image through an appropriate wardrobe. Even if you resent it bitterly — invest in your wardrobe — you are investing in your future.

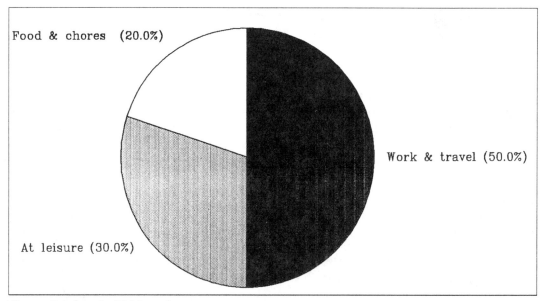

Figure 5.4 *A typical 24-hour day*

WARDROBE MANAGEMENT

Getting yourself and your wardrobe organized so that you know what you've got, which are the successful items and where the weaknesses are, is a first step to managing your clothes rather than letting them control you. Very few of us have the opportunity to start all over again with our business wardrobe, or with our lives, for that matter. The sensible thing to do is to make a plan that utilizes what you've got.

The `Essential Units' wardrobe plan

- The most important aspect about the Essential Units wardrobe plan is that it is *small*.
- Every item should be carefully chosen so that everything matches. Think about every item in the context of:
    Colour – Fabric – Shape and Style – Function.
- Spend time identifying what are the essentials for your needs. Build on these basic units. When you are sure what really suits you and what works in reality then you can gradually add further items to the basics.
- With care and flair, each item in the essential units wardrobe will fit with any other, like interchangeable pieces of an interlocking puzzle.
- Like most efficient systems, the essential units system is *simple*. The hard work goes into the thinking, planning and research stages. The rewards lie in the confidence that comes from the results of a well-managed investment. It is possible to look good on a daily basis with the minimum of fuss.

Action plan

- Identify existing basics.
- Identify the 'gaps'.
- Decide on appropriate colour scheme — which basic neutrals, which accents.
- Decide on a budget.
- Plan a time scale.
- Do your research — find out what is available in your size, price range, preferred style, best colours, likely labels.

- Shop. Whether you are going to a department store or shopping by mail order, set aside enough time to do the job properly. Follow up window-shopping with serious buying.
- Look for the right accessories that are going to add style and flair.

Colour

- A wardrobe based on the essential unit idea works best when planned for a very restricted colour scheme. Two, or at the most, three colours that suit you and complement each other form the basics. Highlight these with one or more accent colours used in small quantities.
- Apply the same rules of a restricted colour scheme to underwear, jewellery and accessories.
- Colours can be chosen from your best neutrals, either light, medium or dark, for a conservative look, or built up from stronger, brighter colours for a more creative or informal look.
- Add from as wide a range of accents as you like.

Fabric

- In temperate climates it is not usually necessary to have completely different wardrobes for the seasons of the year. In most cases it is enough to put together outfits consisting of medium-weight fabrics in natural fibres such as wool, cotton, linen or silk and put on or take off the layers according to the temperature.
- If the summers get hotter and the winters get colder, you may have to consider developing significantly different capsule wardrobes for the changing seasons. However, the layering technique using trans-seasonal fabrics and garments will reduce the need for seasonal wardrobes.
- Contrasting textures are more useful than a mixture of patterns that cannot be worn together.

Shape and style

- Each essential unit should be of a flattering style and silhouette. Every piece should work for its keep. You cannot afford any passengers.

- Each piece should have the capability of being worn over, under or with any other piece.
- Every combination should maintain a good line and flatter the appearance.

Function

- Decide what the units are for. Are they solely for work or will they double as off-duty clothes?
- Each item in the essential units wardrobe should be chosen for a particular purpose but you will get more wear from items that serve more than one purpose: office, dinner, conference or presentation.
- Successful, versatile items can be used to create new satellite wardrobes with different functions.

Ten ways to make your business wardrobe more effective

It is said that we wear 15 per cent of our clothes 85 per cent of the time. The key to a successful wardrobe is to be well organized, have fewer clothes and be ruthless about the clothes that are not earning their keep. If being organized does not come naturally a few practical hints might help:

- Look at the eight to ten garments you wear more often than any of the others. What makes them so popular? Once you can analyze why they are successful you can repeat the success and make fewer mistakes.
- Look at the items you don't wear so often, or not at all. What is the matter with each of them? You probably don't wear them for one of these reasons:
  — it doesn't fit;
  — it's the wrong colour;
  — it's not really 'you';
  — it's out of fashion;
  — you don't like it any more but it's too good to throw away;
  — you are saving it for 'best'.
Don't let it hang there making you feel guilty for wasting the money,

or a fool for making the mistake. Get rid of it. No, it won't come back into fashion and if it does it won't look the same next time round.

- Have six-monthly sort outs. Get everything out of the wardrobe(s) and cupboard(s) and put it round the room. Keep your real favourites to one side and take a ruthless look at the rest. Some will be OK with a bit of attention, some need to go in a black bin bag, some could be offered to a friend or someone in the family who admires them. Consider offering the good quality, little worn garments for sale in a dress exchange. This mainly applies to women's clothes but there are also some places for men. The rest can go to a jumble sale or charity shop (it would be a kindness not to cut off buttons or unpick zips).
- Identify the gaps this exercise has left. Make a shopping list. Stick to it!
- Try to recognize those mistakes you keep repeating and avoid them in the future:
  — the bargain you never wear;
  — the skirt that is waiting for 'when I lose weight';
  — the jacket that looked terrific on someone else;
  — the outfit bought in a hurry because you were desperate for something for a special occasion;
  — the outfit you bought to cheer yourself up and have never worn;
  — the tie that your mother/sister/girlfriend bought that you hate but keep because you don't like to throw it away in case you offend her; don't let other people buy you ties (or anything else for that matter) unless you admire their taste. Say that you have to abide by a very strict dress code at work and must be responsible for your own wardrobe.
- Remember the *Rule of Three*. Before you buy something new, consider whether it will:
  — go with *three* things you already have;
  — can be worn for *three* different kinds of event;
  — could be worn for *three* seasons.
- There is also the *Cost Per Wearing* factor—*CPW*. Imagine you have bought a suit for work for £250. You wear it once a week for a year.

Divide £250 by 52 and you have:

$$\frac{250}{52} = \text{CPW } 4.80$$

You might at the same time have bought a silk shirt in the sale for £35 but have only been able to find an opportunity to wear it twice. The CPW factor looks like this:

$$\frac{35}{2} = \text{CPW } 17.5$$

Look at your existing wardrobe and apply the CPW factor. You may be in for a few surprises. Aim for a CPW factor that is as low as possible.

- Don't be tempted by something merely 'useful' — it's likely to be boring as well. Only buy something when you can honestly answer 'yes' to these two questions:
  — Is it appropriate for my professional image?
  — Does it make me look terrific?
- Don't be afraid to have minor alterations done. Skirts and trousers can be made narrower or wider and their hems are easily shortened, as are sleeves. The cost is likely to be only a fraction of the purchase price but will make such a difference.
- Keep your clothes *visible* — you won't wear what you can't see.

WARDROBE MAINTENANCE

- Keep everything cleaned, pressed, mended and stored properly. You'll then have more choice and fewer panics. Air outer clothes outside the wardrobe overnight, other clothes go in the linen basket.
- Storage: give everything enough room so that it doesn't get creased or squashed.
- Hangers: buy the correct hanger for the job:
  — skirts need to be supported from the waistband, not hung by those little stringy loops;
  — suit jackets need a strong wooden or padded hanger;
  — blouses in fine fabrics need soft padded hangers;
  — trousers should be either hung upside down with the hems gripped in rubber or folded over a padded bar;
  — shoes need shoe trees to help them stay in shape.

- Use soft cotton gloves when putting on special tights to avoid snagging them.
- Allow for dry-cleaning and repairs in your clothing budget.
- Jackets, trousers and skirts should rest and relax between wearings.
- Any garment that touches your skin should be washed before it is worn again.
- Allow time for washing and ironing. Be realistic about your preference and temperament. Do you like ironing or not? A dozen beautiful cotton shirts need a lot of tender loving care. Pay to have them laundered or ironed if you resent doing it yourself or are not prepared to learn.
- Have a clothes brush handy and something to remove lint, fluff and cat's hairs. Sellotape wrapped round the fingers, sticky side out, works well.

Quality control

If it doesn't come naturally you may not have acquired the skill of recognizing a good fit and a high standard of construction. So, how do you tell a well-made garment? Here is a checklist for successful do-it-yourself quality control.

Start on the inside:

- Seam allowances should be at least half an inch (1.5cm).
- Seams should be finished with zig-zag or overlock stitch in a matching colour thread. Avoid pinked seams or raw edges.
- The interfacings should be smooth and wrinkle-free and sit flat against the garment without pulling. Look carefully at collar, cuffs, revers and pockets.
- Hems should be finished with tape or overlocked with a matching thread that does not show on the right side. A visible machine hem will not do except in special circumstances such as a design element, on fine jersey or a full circular skirt.
- Good quality skirts, trousers and jackets always have a lining, at least for half their length, unless the current look is lightweight and unstructured or designed to be transparent.
- Try this test — hold a side seam up to the light and gently pull apart

— if you can see large gaps in the stitching then too few stitches per inch have been used and the garment will not wear well.

Check the outside:

- Prints, checks and stripes should match at all seams including collars, pockets and front openings.
- There should be no loose threads anywhere.
- Any topstitching should be straight and even.
- Pockets should lie flat and be sewn on straight.
- Buttons should be a good colour match for the fabric and the correct size for the buttonhole.
- Buttonholes should be straight and accurate with no loose threads.
- The zip should lie flat and be a good colour match for the garment.
- If the quality of the garment is otherwise good but spoilt by an inferior belt and buttons, a quality look can be restored by replacing them with buttons made from bone, metal, pearl, leather or wood.
- Skirts and trousers have greater hanger appeal if displayed with a belt at the waist-line. These are seldom of good quality so you get a classier look by discarding the belt in favour of a good one of your own.

BUDGET

Budget is an attitude of mind. My experience is that most people spend money according to what they are prepared to spend not on what they can afford. You could afford £275 on a suit but resent money spent on anything outside home and family interests. I could afford to spend £45 on a new duvet cover and pillow cases but consider it an outrageous sum. The same day I could spend the same amount on a meal for two and consider the money well spent and without a thing to show for it.

As a rough guide, allow two weeks' salary for a year's business wardrobe. If you earn £25,000 it is not unreasonable to allow £1,000 for major and minor items.

BUILDING AN APPROPRIATE BUSINESS WARDROBE

Coco Chanel believed that above all else, clothes should be logical. Consider the logic of your business wardrobe and clothing needs. Everyone needs a formal business suit in a conservative cut and colour for the most formal aspects of their working life — interviews, presentations and so on. After that it is simply a question of having the right number of garments — tops, middles and bottoms, plus their accessories — so that you have a logical, simple, co-ordinated system that will never let you down.

C H A P T E R

PERSONAL STYLE

INDIVIDUAL IMAGE

Many people I work with have an unfocused sense of personal style. They lack confidence about what they should be wearing and in many cases simply don't know what they like. They want to meet the expectations of the organization but don't want to sacrifice their integrity. My clients are highly qualified, well-educated professionals. Whatever their specialism, they voice similar concerns. Women fear that if they wear make-up, are well groomed and dress stylishly they will run the risk of being dubbed an 'executive trollop'. If they make no concessions to image at all they are perceived as unsophisticated, lesbian or left wing. The dilemma for both men and women is how to find a suitable way of demonstrating individuality, leadership and creativity within the guidelines of conventional business dress. Most of us know instinctively what we prefer to wear and have also developed some sense of what is appropriate for different occasions. At the same time we are able to recognize that what we really like has been eroded by habit, laziness, the needs of the job, other people's taste or unhelpful or pushy shop assistants. What we don't seem able to do is mould it all together to create our own individual, professional image.

Style sulk

A young finance director was trapped in the usual accountant's uniform of navy suit, striped shirt and club tie. I guessed that this was not his preferred style as he was so uncomfortable in it. He felt obliged to wear formal clothes at his level in his organization. He was wearing what was required but was doing so with the least possible grace and style. I asked him what his favourite off-duty garment was. His eyes lit up, 'My black leather jacket,' he said. We discovered that he had the capacity for stylish dressing off-duty but was not transferring his skill across to his business wardrobe. He was doing a 'style sulk'. If he couldn't do it his way then he wouldn't do it at all. He couldn't wear his leather jacket to work, but he did climb out of the strait-jacket of his current business image and move towards a more masculine, dramatic look in which he felt more at home. He still wears suits but the cut is more elegant and the accessories more individual.

The white shirt test

If you asked a roomful of female friends and colleagues (women are more willing to play this game than men) to put on the same white shirt and personalize it with a few limited accessories to reflect their taste and style, the results would fall into these categories.

Classic. Collar open, row of pearls showing, tucked in to skirt or trousers.
Avant-garde. Buttons left open, wrapped round the waist, tying the shirt tails at the front, cuffs left open and hanging.
Masculine. Neck closed, fastened with a small brooch or scarf, cuffs done up, cufflinks.
Feminine. Neck open, chiffon scarf draped round neck-line, tucked in at waist.
Uncluttered. Neck open, cuffs closed, hanging straight outside skirt or trousers.
Decorated. Collar up, large brooch at neck, clip on buttons to cover existing buttons, tucked in to skirt or trousers waistline then covered with a belt.
Natural. Collar undone, sleeves rolled up, cotton scarf at neck.
Glamorous. Buttons undone, collar up, sleeves pushed up, row of bracelets up one arm, belted over skirt or trousers.

Most women respond instinctively and work with what's available to reflect their style. If you make the exercise more sophisticated and ask the same people to personalize a whole business wardrobe the less confident will go to pieces.

STYLE PREFERENCE EXERCISE

The following exercise is designed to:

- Help you to decide what you really like.
- Analyze how appropriate your preference is within the guidelines of what is acceptable for the job.
- Show how you can transfer elements of your preferred style to the required style for the job.

The aim of the exercise is to reveal your true preferences. It is presented as a set of opposites using the extremes of style characteristics. Opposites can live together in one person but sometimes the stronger style wins. The drab Puritans won an eventual victory over the gaudy Cavaliers. The

Figure 6.1 *Style preference (cartoon by Bestie)*

Puritans wore a quiet style of dress with no colour, only black and white, cut on simple lines with no adornment. In contrast the Cavalier style was colourful, extravagant and highly decorative.

There is a contemporary parallel in the war between the 'Voluptuaries' and 'Cerebrals' as Brenda Polan of *The Times* observed. Giorgio Armani is the leader of the Cerebrals. He produces minimalist, classy, classic clothes in neutral colours. Gianni Versace, a 'body exposing fantasist' who insists that 'real women don't wear beige', flies the flag for the Voluptuaries. There are women who enjoy the extremes of both styles and after wearing an Armani suit (or Armani style suit) in a meeting will flaunt their assets in a Dolce and Gabbano bustier and Versace jeans at a club. Which do you prefer — or don't you know? Use this exercise to confirm or wake up your preferences.

Step 1

Looking at Figure 6.2 mark a point along the line that shows how far the strength of your preference leans towards one of the extremes. In some cases you might mark the limits for both extremes. Some people prefer an uncluttered look for day and a decorated look for evening. They would make their mark at the extreme left at 'uncluttered' as well as at the extreme right for 'decorated'. You wouldn't do this unless your tastes were extreme. Some people choose to be very polished or glamorous for work and adopt a natural look for off-duty. If you are a person of

Classic	Avant–garde
Masculine	Feminine
Uncluttered	Decorated
Natural	Glamorous
Neat and tidy	Chaotic
Plain	Patterns
Neutral	Colours
Pastels	Earthy colours
Tailored	Loose

Figure 6.2 *Personal style*

extremes and opposites in taste, dress and behaviour your chart could have one or more loops in it. You should consider the problems of value judgements — tidiness and the masculine elements have higher values in professional dressing than untidiness and femininity.

Interpret the result

- If you sometimes prefer one look and sometimes another or you can't decide between the extremes, your personal style will lack focus. A straight line through the centre indicates the most boring, least stylish look.
- A straight line down the left-hand side could indicate an uncompromising, boring, understated look which on a woman could be misunderstood as being unworldly unless it's done in very good taste.
- A straight line down the right-hand side would indicate an alarming and visually disturbing look. It is theatrical and highly expressive and could be interpreted as the wearer being obsessed with their appearance.
- Strong personalities with bold ideas will have straight lines at the far right or left. They need to remind themselves that extreme looks can be intimidating and could indicate arrogance and selfishness.
- An interesting and expressive look is usually indicated by a wavy line.
- A traditional business look is created where the left side predominates.

Step 2

We all have elements of all the characteristics to some degree. One of them is likely to predominate. Decide which characteristic is most *you*. When you have selected your preferred style, you have to decide whether, in essence, it is appropriate for the image you want to project in your job. If it is appropriate, there follows advice on how to project the essence of your style and make it consistent. If it isn't, there is advice on how to hold on to the essentials of your look so that you feel right but can adapt it to meet your business image requirements. Read the following section right through before going on to Step 3 in the next section.

PRIMARY STYLE CHARACTERISTICS

Classic: *a model of its kind, balanced, formal, restrained, regular, traditional or simple in style*

A classic dresser often has classical physique and features. They are typically of medium height with even, well-balanced features, well-proportioned body and well-groomed. They cannot tolerate extremes and are conservative in both style and outlook. Classic good looks are needed to wear severely classic clothes unrelieved by personal interpretation. A classic dresser looks best in all kinds of classic garments and styles from an Establishment business suit to black leather jacket, Levis and white T-shirt.

Colour. Neutral colours, subtle colours.

Fabric. Looks good in natural fibres: linen, silk, cotton, wool, good quality fabrics that tailor well and hang away from the body and do not cling or reveal the body; wool crepe, smooth wool gaberdine, cashmere, fine-knitted jersey in cotton or wool, cavalry twill, fine corduroy, lightweight flannel, satin, velvet, subtle brocade, brushed cotton, medium-weight denim, men's shirtings and suitings used for women's wear.

Texture. Not so good in heavy or hairy textures.

Pattern. Stylized, formal, geometric prints, even repeat patterns not splashes or daubs, paisley in favour of floral, small to medium dots, narrow to medium conservative stripes in favour of overscale.

Style plus. Can appear elegant and well-dressed and achieve an expensive and classy look without using the expensive versions.

Style minus. Can be boring, too conservative, not prepared to experiment with colour, style or quality.

Personal twist
- Keep to classic cut and colour but introduce more avant-garde accessories.
- Keep to classic cut but introduce fashion or fun colours.
- Keep to classic cut and colour but introduce interesting cloth and texture.
- Keep to classic colours but introduce more fashion forward, exaggerated style lines.

Avant-garde: *from the French, vanguard; leaders in new movements, ideas; an intelligentsia that develops new or experimental concepts*

As a true stylist your first rule is that when you see the wrong people wearing it, you move on. You enjoy wearing what most people are not wearing – yet! You belong with the style leaders. It is important for this kind of dresser to wear styles before they reach the general consumer. As soon as the look hits the high street or preferably before then, they have moved on to something else. This kind of dresser needs an audience.

Colour. All-black or all-white always make a strong statement, whatever the chosen style.

Fabric. Womenswear fabrics used for menswear, for example chiffon or lace; fabrics associated with one use used for another such as silver lamé for a boiler-suit or rubber, horse-blankets, plastic sheeting used for outerwear.

Texture. De-constructing fabrics, shredding, slashing, wearing them inside-out, fabrics constructed from discarded items — bottle caps, phone cards, orange fruit netting.

Pattern. Either looking back to an era that everyone else thinks is ugly, for example 1950s kitsch, or looking forward to new technology, as in welded seams.

Style plus. Can be seen as clever and adventurous, can attract admiration from conservative colleagues.

Style minus. An extreme avant-garde style can be seen as anarchic or difficult and attracts ridicule or envy.

Personal twist

- If this is your preferred style, wear your most conservative look for work but make as strong a statement at top and bottom (hair style, make-up, shoes) as you feel you can get away with.
- play up the juxtaposition of unexpected items or garments worn with a traditional business wardrobe.

Masculine: *having qualities regarded as characteristic of men and boys*

In design terms masculine refers to darker colours, straighter lines, angles, crisper textures.

Colour. Navy, charcoal, pine green, burgundy, dark chocolate.

Fabric. Gaberdine, flannel, fine worsted — any fabric associated with traditional men's clothing.

Texture. Smooth or rugged, not in between.

Pattern. Stripes, herringbone, tartan, Prince of Wales check.

Style plus. Whether worn by a man or a woman, masculine design elements are perceived as professional, sober and business-like.

Style minus. In its extreme interpretation, can look intimidating when worn by a woman or severe and unapproachable when worn by a man.

Personal twist

- Use a touch of the stylistic opposite — soft colours for ties and shirts for men. Softer hair, daintier shoes, lighter colours for women.
- For women — make sure that garments and accessories have just a touch of masculine styling rather than borrow wholesale from the man's wardrobe.

Feminine: *having qualities regarded as characteristic of women and girls*

In design terms feminine means using lighter colours, flowing lines, curves, soft textures.

Colour. Bold brights or faded, gentle, soft tones.

Fabric. Black velvet, white lace, chiffon, voile, angora, soft silks, crepe de Chine, broderie anglaise, organza, soft rayon, fine cotton jersey.

Texture. Transparent, floating, fabrics that use embroidery, smocking or quilting.

Pattern: Floral prints, small Victorian prints and patterns, narrow blended stripes, watercolour wash abstract prints, faded cotton chintz.

Style plus. Looks good in antique or period clothes, in romantic styles, fragile jewellery, lace, sashes, hats, soft bows, classic clothes in lighter colours and softer fabrics, soft clinging and floating in favour of crisp, starchy or heavier versions.

Style minus. Can be too 'girly' on women, too effeminate on men. There is the problem of not being taken seriously — if the clothes are frilly and fluffy so might the thinking be. Men who enjoy the feminine design elements of dress will find their style best appreciated in a female environment. Pink shirt, interesting texture jacket, hand printed silk tie will be appropriate in all but the most conservative environments. Crisp tailoring or minimal decoration can bring this look to an acceptable level of professional dressing. There is still plenty of room for feminine interpretation in hair style and shoes.

Personal twist
- Use a touch of its stylistic opposite (masculine) and use just one masculine element.
- Make sure that every aspect of the outfit has one of the feminine design elements even if it doesn't go all the way.

Uncluttered: *few things, in order, not scattered*

To take an uncluttered style to the limit means to go for stark simplicity, minimalism; removing all decoration, no buttons, minimal accessories; concentrating on simple lines and neutral colours.

Colour. Cool neutrals in dark, medium or light tones such as black, navy, grey, rose brown, taupe, string, beige, ivory, off-white worn to blend — cream/porridge/white or to provide contrast — charcoal grey/off-white.

Fabric. Modern or traditional fabrics, medium to heavy weight, that don't flow or swing. Not linen or stone-washed silk because they crumple and distract from the simple line.

Texture. Flat, smooth surface.

Pattern. Self-pattern, or no pattern.

Style plus. Looks contemporary, chic, European, intellectual.

Style minus. Can be boring, can be stark, message of no holds barred.

Personal twist
- Use a monochromatic colour scheme using contrasting texture for visual interest.
- Use one piece as a focal point: single button, asymmetric cut, circular tie-pin.

Decorated: *adorned, richly ornamented*

In its extreme form can be visually exciting or a nightmare. Every aspect of appearance is embellished. Women: hair decorations, slides, combs and a scrunch in the hair, earrings, decorated spectacles, chain for spectacles, lavish make-up, charm bracelet, wrist-watch with decorative detail, clip-on buttons, pocket flaps, embroidery on blouse, stitching detail, embroidered tote bag, bows on shoes. Men: shirt, suit and tie all in different patterns and textures, waistcoat with decorative buttons, fob watch and chain, cufflinks, patterned socks, subtle and clever when done well, headache-making when not.

Colour. Any.

Fabric. Any.

Texture. Anything with surface texture or embellishment, crushed velvet, devorée, wool, self-patterned cottons, Jacquard weave, watered silk.

Pattern. Anything.

Style plus. Interesting to look at, often wears 'conversation pieces'. Willing to spend time looking for the right pieces.

Style minus. Doesn't know when to stop, over matches colour schemes, particularly at weddings, for example blue dress with white collar has blue and white shell buttons, a white hat with blue veiling, navy shoes with white toe cap, one row of blue beads, one row of white beads, navy handbag with white trim and white tights with a little navy bow at the ankle.

Personal twist

- Keep to a tightly controlled colour scheme or stick to a theme, for example squares, African, or flowers.
- Always have one visual resting place so that the decoration is more effective.

Natural: *not artificial, free from affectation*

A natural type is typically of athletic build, enjoys informality and being casual.

Colour. Plain colours, conservative palette, 'countryside' such as browns and greens, herbs not spices, nothing to frighten the animals, nautical combinations of blues and whites.

Fabric. Natural fibres, tweeds, hand-woven fabrics, medium to heavy weight corduroy, chambray, brushed cotton, quilted fabrics, tartan, denim, Aertex, raw silk gabardine.

Texture. Matt surface, not shiny or theatrical fabrics.

Pattern. Small checks eg gingham, over-check, Tattersall check, fairisle, Argyle tartan, narrow stripes, small-scale paisleys.

Style plus. Looks good in sports clothes: sailing, tennis, track suits, gym or workout gear, shorts, tee shirts; the very English outdoors country look—cable-knit jumpers, sweaters, Guernsey pullovers, brogues, Barbour jacket, wellington boots, cords.

Style minus. Requires comfort before chic, ignores the needs of the event or the job, therefore has a tendency to be under-dressed. The casual style that a natural wears so well, can easily become sloppy or scruffy. Dressing up for a formal event such as an interview or special occasion such as a wedding can cause anxieties resulting in the chosen outfit looking uncomfortable and unrelated to the wearer. Women can be shy about revealing femininity or uncomfortable about 'dressing up'. Men and women can look and feel uncomfortable in formal clothes if cut and texture are not right for them.

Personal twist
- Go all out for the country gent or Sloane look with all the details.
- Well-cut hair in terrific condition that always looks the same and needs minimum maintenance.
- Fresh clean skin, skin fitness routine, healthy look.
- Give professional dressing a nautical flavour using navy and white. Crisp white shirt with navy blazer, navy loafers and tartan skirt for women, beige cavalry twills or grey flannels for men.
- A navy business suit cut for comfort in an easy-care fabric that will thrive on neglect, worn with blue cotton twill shirt and club or silk tie for men, status scarf for women.

Glamorous: *seemingly mysterious and elusive fascination or allure, bewitching charm*

A glamorous or polished look can be attractive, glossy, artificial. A noticeable style, some people give it a film-star quality. Often a dramatic dresser, they feel at home in the extremes of stark simplicity, or clutter raised to the level of an art form. The look is not easily arrived at but is born of an intense interest in clothes and style and objects but not necessarily in self. Typically, they present an understated style touched by bold strokes.

Colour. Strong, deep and rich or white and pale.
Fabric. Plain, but of the very best quality or ornate brocades, cashmere, printed velvet.
Texture. Surface decoration, embellishment, ethnic embroidery.
Pattern. Bold geometrics, highly stylized abstracts, rich colourways.
Style plus. Always interesting to look at, can be relied upon to dress up

for a special occasion, in a conservative profession can sweep in and knock the breath out of stuffy colleagues or clients.

Style minus. Worn with confidence verging on arrogance, this look can be intimidating. The wearer has difficulty making compromises for appropriate professional dressing. They fail to realize that what they wear affects others as well as themselves.

Personal twist.
- Already a highly personal style.
- Stunning colour and/or texture, simple cut.
- One piece of oversized designer jewellery for women.
- Extreme cut in conservative colour for women.
- Embroidered waistcoat for men.
- Hand-woven cloth for jacket for men or women.
- Distinctive hat, and boots worn when travelling.

SECONDARY STYLE CHARACTERISTICS

Neat and tidy

Over-concern with hygiene and order in clothing (being too neat and tidy) suggests anal-retentive types. A perfectionist can be a pleasure to look at but also runs the risk of appearing fussy and obsessive. Neatness, tidiness and high standards of grooming and hygiene are expected from uniform and quasi-uniform wearers—commissionaires, nurses or air-line pilots. Lack of proper order in dressing, particularly in uniform, suggests lack of discipline or potential lack of discipline and by association lack of professional competence.

Chaotic

On the other hand, too much chaos can be charming or alarming. A chaotic dress style can be a sign of a disordered mind. As an example, think of patients from mental health care institutions in clothes that don't match, don't fit, are not well cared for, odd socks, buttons done up incorrectly. This is usually for two reasons: (*a*) because they have no sense of what is 'right' and (*b*) the people who care for them don't see dress as a priority and ignore the link between dress and self-esteem. The stereotypical absent-minded professor wears frayed cuffs, worn out woolly cardigans, mismatched colours and textures and a variety of interesting stains on tie and shirt front.

Step 3

When you have decided on your primary style characteristic, use the *Personal twist* section of that characteristic and consider ways of emphasizing your preferred look. If it is out of focus, this step should enable you to make a clearer style statement. If your style is making too strong a statement for the dominant culture of your firm or profession, it will give you ideas for pulling back a little.

Where is the best arena for your style?

Every profession has a set of formal or informal expectations about what its practitioners will wear. Every business has stereotypes or at least a series of working role models for new entrants to emulate. Large organizations employ professionals across all business specialisms from accounts to marketing, and catering to production. The dominant dress code can change from department to department. Where will your style fit best?

Occupations such as the law, accountancy, finance or management consultancy, particularly those based in the City of London or Wall Street, still require partners to wear only formal business clothes. This level of dress is required at all times regardless of who they are meeting and in whatever part of the country. A company with a creative end-product such as an avant-garde film company might need a conservatively dressed accountant to ground them and give them credibility. A well-established management consultancy working with blue-chip clients might need a more avant-garde finance manager to give them the status of creative business thinkers.

In the public sector, in the NHS for example, the dominant culture varies widely from area to area and specialism to specialism. NHS Trusts are encouraged to think of themselves as a business and be more business-like in the way they operate. This can lead to a conflict between managers who want to go along this route and established clinicians and support staff who see their primary responsibility as providing patient care, not to get done up like a dog's dinner. This attitude is supported by recent IPM research indicating that new graduates entering management in the 1990s want to work in the caring professions where they perceive their personal style to be unimportant, rather than in finance, computers and retail where an appropriate business image counts.

Education and Social Services don't place much emphasis on dress although I regularly meet exceptions. Casual wear is common among hands-on professionals such as social workers. 'Visiting people's homes you don't want to attract attention or wear anything too good because you don't know what you might have to sit on — or in.' In this kind of culture, a professional wearing smart clothes, even at executive level, is perceived as slightly suspect.

The Civil Service is a huge and complex organization with a complex internal culture to match. Each department and layers of each department have their own rules which are difficult for an outsider and sometimes an insider to penetrate.

In the private sector, each industry has internal standards of dress and it is not possible to make helpful generalizations, but if your personal style is important to you, you will always be unhappy in an environment that does not encourage personal expression.

Who is the best audience for your style?

Any management job is going to involve daily contact with people, so who is going to be most responsive to your personal style?

Women with all female colleagues
In a conservative environment staffed mainly by women, there are plenty of opportunities for a daily fashion parade if the work itself is rather boring. In a creative environment like a PR fashion company a strong personal style is taken for granted and won't attract overt comments. It is the clients' style that provides a constant source for comment.

Women with all male colleagues
A woman in a predominantly male environment, in a conservative business such as law for example, can either choose to dress like one of the boys or choose the 'butterfly' option. The female equivalent of the dark suit and white shirt worn with a tie substitute will blend in with men's business suits. Bright colours, flowing hair and soft fabrics will show up

like a butterfly in a room full of moths. An overt, hard-edged feminine style in male company implies the female would consume her male colleagues in time of trouble.

Men with all female colleagues

As the only man you can indulge in creative and interesting clothes as this is the best environment for your appearance to attract notice and provoke comment.

Men with all male colleagues

This is the least likely scenario for daily comment on clothes and style, although man-to-man conversations are heard about best places to have shirts made and where to locate good silk ties when on holiday in Italy.

> As a fairly democractic organization we are not keen on the 'tall poppy' syndrome. However, in the section that I head up, what I'm looking for is a person's ability to number-crunch — so it doesn't matter what they wear inside the building. Although, they might have a problem when it came to internal promotion.
>
> Jeff Evans, banking consultant, interviewed 1993

LACK OF STYLE — WHOSE FAULT IS IT?

Social trends

Social, political and economic trends undoubtedly influence what we wear. The world of work has been transforming itself from rigid conformity to New Age *laissez faire*. There is an inescapable move towards a more informal approach to life. There is a trend, by no means universal as yet, of dressing down, on and off-duty. In the so-called caring 90s, short, sharp suits highlighted with gold jewellery are being overtaken by a form of business scruffiness. So now we have the style-conscious manager struggling between the polarization of tough professional and caring colleague.

The fashion factor

Any new trend, whether it is in fashion or management theory, will have its enthusiastic supporters and its quota of the suspicious. Being fashion forward in your personal style will be viewed according to where your audience is placed on the ladder of response to new ideas.

Innovators
make the new moves, create the changes

Early acceptors
as soon as they see a new idea they will try it out

Late acceptors
are willing to take a risk after others have taken the first step

Early majority
need to see the proof and the reality before they commit themselves

Late majority
need to have long-term experience before they feel secure enough to try it out, by which time it's nearly out of fashion

Laggards
pick up the idea by its coat-tails as it's flying away

Rejectors
`Over my dead body'

Figure 6.3 *Ladder of response*

By the time the innovators have rejected black leggings (or TQM,[*] empowerment or outdoor learning) the late majority are just beginning to see that they look quite good after all.

Fashion interprets current social, political and economic trends and serves up our own era in the form of clothes. Sometimes we are not ready for what is served. The fashion continuum might include at any one time Mid-America 'home-on-the-range', Principal Boys, Dandies and bandaged cadavers. The fashion industry offers vast consumer choice, especially to women, and so there are plenty of opportunities for errors of judgement. Fashion has always been an easy target for humorists from *Punch* to the robust observations of my local greengrocer. This means

---

[*]   Total Quality Management

that the style-conscious have to brave the flak from the conservative and the boorish. Fashion editors are interested in what will make a good visual 'story', not in guiding their readers through a debate about personal style.

Insufficient role models

'No style please, we're British!' Finance and law are the heartland of Establishment style; the power lies with these men so they remain sartorial role models. Or do they? Professional men have more role models than women but fewer sartorial choices. Traditional professional dress for men that apes Establishment dressing is comparatively static and varies only in small degrees from year to year and company to company. There are other possible role models — the Italians maybe? Roz Mac-Leod, fashion editor of *Menswear* magazine thinks so, 'The Italians wear jackets, trousers and suede shoes in the office. Until recently, only media and creative types have been able to get away with that in Britain. But that's all changing now.' Italians from sophisticated cities dress well anyway. Whatever they wear, they make sure they are co-ordinated and well presented.

The Americans? Charles Jennings has a theory about the way forward through corporate delinquency, 'Apple Computers in California is more like a college campus than a temple of capitalism.' David Dworkin arrived from Miami to sort out the troubles of the Storehouse retailing group and appeared at meetings in jeans and sweaters. Bill Gates the Microsoft billionaire '... parades round his fiefdom in scuffed loafers, gone-at-the-knee chinos and badly ironed sweatshirts — a living picture of corporate delinquency'.

Are there role models closer to home? Maybe Richard Branson, the sweater-wearing chairman of Virgin Atlantic, represents the future? Lord King, the former chairman of British Airways, would find that difficult: 'If Richard Branson had worn a pair of steel rimmed glasses [and] a double breasted suit, and shaved off his beard, I would have taken him seriously. As it was I couldn't.'

Negative conditioning

Many professionals, especially those from academic backgrounds, learn that self-presentation skills are vain, frivolous and unnecessary. An intellectually superior attitude to clothes has resulted in a low level of style awareness. A lack of street cred means that they end up looking dowdy, uncomfortable or simply boring. They have no pleasure and no pride in their appearance. They are unaware that the way they dress is inappropriate for the demands of the more public aspects of their work.

Parents have a lot to answer for, especially mothers — and I speak as one. For some of us, our only concern is that our children should be neat, clean and respectable. We want to dress them up as little adults. In contrast, other parents opt out of an interest in their children's clothing altogether and from a very early age allow their children to dictate to them about what they will wear. Without supervision or feedback the result is style anarchy. Putting children into school uniform solves some problems but creates others. Unless they receive positive feedback during their early years, children's negative feelings about clothes won't have been resolved by the time they have to make decisions about business dress. Other people's taste can act negatively on a developing sense of style. When self-esteem is low we allow partners, shop assistants, parents, children, bosses and friends to undermine our choices. Habit, laziness, lack of funds and the needs of the job all contribute negatively to an expression of self through personal style.

Lack of style training

Dressing well is not a skill that we inherit. Even so, people are somehow expected to know the rules. Because we don't have a recent history of intellectual discussion about style and clothing we are embarrassed to consider it as a serious topic for debate, let alone for training. What discussion there might be is done by women and trivialized by men. Men overheard discussing clothes are considered peculiar. Not everyone is naturally good with clothes. They have no sense of what is appropriate or aesthetically pleasing. Why don't they discuss it or ask for help? Why do they persist in the Puritan notion that an interest in either the psychological, aesthetic or symbolic aspects of dress is trivial and stands on the periphery of life? The current move towards informality means that there are many people who don't know the elements of basic design or the rules of formal dressing. Maybe its time for a series of Personal Style classes to be run alongside the Social Skills programme in the school curriculum.

7

WHAT TO WEAR FOR WHAT

People often ask my advice about what to wear for important occasions, particularly those that involve an element of presenting to an audience. In order to help people to dress appropriately for an event, particularly one that involves public speaking, I need to be briefed in some detail about the event: who is going to be there and why the speakers were invited. The advice offered here applies to the three most common requests and is relevant to a range of formal and informal public presentations.

DRESS FOR THE EVENT

What to wear for a job interview

- Don't advertise what you can't deliver.
- You are there to see whether you will fit in, so you need to come across naturally and be your professional best. If you know you really want the job, you need to arrive looking as though you already belong. The interviewer(s) is probably looking, unconsciously, for someone who is already wearing the 'team strip'.
- Arrive looking good, you don't know who you might meet on the way in.
- Convention has it that both sides wear their best suit for a formal interview.

- For manual or technical work, media or social services, wearing casual clothes is usually acceptable.
- For almost anything else, the expectation on both sides is the dark suit for men and something fairly conservative for women, although the range of acceptable alternatives is greater for women. The trick is to project the best possible 'you' and let your personal style make its mark within the boundaries of interview conventions. See Chapter 6 for some ideas.
- An important interview is not the time to try out a new look or brand new garments. Aim for physical comfort as well as style.
- Grooming has to be spot on. See Chapter 3: Business Grooming Strategy.
- If you do not get appointed ask for feedback. If your experience and qualifications were ideal, ask if the problem was anything to do with your personal presentation style. Listen carefully and say 'thank you' whether you like what you hear or not. If there is something you can change, learn how to change it. If you can't or won't change you would never have been happy there anyway.

What to wear for television

- Any actor will tell you that the camera either loves you or it doesn't. Either way there are some tricks of the trade that will help if you are a novice with this medium.
- The general rule is 'less is more'.
- A well-defined shoulder-line looks more impressive.
- Avoid fussy detailing at the neck.
- For men, a discreetly-patterned tie comes over better than a bold pattern, even if bold is your usual choice.
- Colour: neutrals will work well; stone, grey, navy and beige, as will the medium-toned blues, greens and mauves. Avoid reds which can 'bleed', and strong contrast such as black and white.
- Avoid stripes and spots and large-scale patterns such as tartans which can 'dance' on screen and be distracting.
- Glasses: a non-reflective coating on the lenses. Avoid tinted or photochromatic lenses; they make you look a bit sinister.
- Make sure you are comfortable.

- If in the studio, take some alternative garments with you if you're not sure how you will come across; take any cosmetics or grooming aids you think you might need. No one will think you are vain, you are just being professional by making sure your screen image is satisfactory.
- If on location, make sure someone checks the weather hasn't ruined your image. Speaking from under a large umbrella looks better than standing huddled and dripping in a mac.
- Go on a media skills course; fund it yourself if necessary.

What to wear for a business presentation

Sales presentations, training seminars, conferences, board meetings, lectures and similar situations are all examples of business presentation.

If you are someone who has an intense physical response to giving a presentation, start by checking out what you have in your wardrobe that is physically suitable. Do you get nervous, sweaty, ice cold hands; do you move about a lot, use arm and hand gestures? When you have sorted out the physical conditions you can then consider the purpose of the presentation, the venue and the audience.

- Stand up with your jacket buttoned and keep it buttoned.
- Avoid jackets, skirts or trousers that are too short or too tight.
- Avoid anything that is likely to come apart from anything else — shirt from trousers, petticoat from skirt.
- A small audience requires a non-threatening presence, especially if they are seated close to you. Wear neutrals with some colour interest in tie or blouse, to focus interest towards your face.
- A large audience requires a more dramatic look and stronger colours. A more exaggerated cut will grab audience attention. Avoid bright or bold patterns as they are too distracting, even from a distance.
- Check your background. A bright blue jacket will look great in front of beige panels but sink into insignificance against blue or another strong colour of the same tone.
- If you have to join a panel on a platform check whether there is a modesty cloth covering the table. The view can be unintentionally entertaining for the audience or deeply embarrassing for the presenter.

PREPARATION AND RESEARCH

I have learnt two things about making presentations:

- Never presume.
- Do your research.

I have learned the hard way. For every success there has been an 'interesting experience'. There was Sheffield in the rain. A long, slow journey from London, in appallingly bad weather. The train arrived late, the taxi driver didn't know where he was going and I hadn't brought the file with the address in. I looked like a drowned rat, and wasn't wearing a 'Platform' outfit because I presumed it was a small informal gathering. The local press were there to meet me and they and the welcoming committee were rightly bemused at my billing as a national speaker.

There was the time I was invited to speak to a local Chamber of Commerce. The venue was a long, low reception room with low level lighting. I made my (mercifully) brief presentation in the dark wearing a dark suit standing on a milk crate.

Yes, I do get invited back and yes, I still misjudge situations, but not nearly so often and when it does go wrong, I have the confidence born of good preparation and experience, so at least the audience doesn't suffer.

You can't expect to project a successful image unless you identify what you want to get out of the situation. This is where research comes in. It doesn't matter how large or small the gathering, or whether it is a formal or informal occasion. Some basic research about what to expect when you get there is vital to your success. The research that helps you to select an appropriate and effective image follows the same rules for preparing a successful verbal presentation. Both involve asking questions to be able to make the appropriate decisions.

EVENT CHECKLIST

You could use this checklist to help you plan your next presentation.

DRESS FOR THE EVENT
CHECKLIST

Audience profile

Who is going to be there?	– all men	☐
	– all women	☐
	– men and women	☐
	– social class	☐
	– age range	☐
	– occupations	☐
	– interests	☐
Expectations	– yours	☐
	– theirs	☐
	– the booking agent's	☐
Venue	– easy to get to	☐
	– familiar	☐
	– travel	☐
	– indoors or out	☐
	– comfort level	☐
	– lighting	☐
	– heating	☐
	– seating arrangements	☐
	– audio/visual needs	☐
	– how many people	☐
	– how arranged	☐
Atmosphere	– formal	☐
	– intimidating	☐
	– friendly	☐
	– casual	☐
	– confrontational	☐
	– hostile	☐
Message	– good news or bad	☐
	– inform	☐
	– educate	☐
	– entertain	☐
	– motivate	☐
	– persuade	☐
Required image	– approachable	☐
	– assertive	☐
	– in authority	☐
	– businesslike	☐
	– communicator	☐
	– creative	☐
	– dynamic	☐
	– elegant	☐
	– enthusiastic	☐
	– negotiator	☐
	– relaxed	☐
	– sensitive	☐
Other conditions	– time of day	☐
	– time of year	☐
	– weather	☐

Figure 7.1 *Research helps to decide on an appropriate image*

ENHANCING THE MESSAGE

Studies have shown that new information is absorbed through a combination of the senses, in roughly these proportions:

Vision	75%
Hearing	13%
Touching	6%
Smelling	3%
Tasting	3%

Subliminal messages are received, primarily, through visual imagery. To create a strong, acceptable image at an important presentation, the chosen colour should:

• be in harmony with the wearer's natural colouring;
• match the role and message of the presentation;
• gain an appropriate response from the audience.

Colours have strong psychological and symbolic meanings in all cultures, but responses to colour vary from culture to culture. You can't separate colour from style and an effective image will depend on the successful combination of the two. People respond strongly to colour, so if you have to wear fairly conservative styling you can project your message a little more clearly through the use of colour. Whatever your individual colour characteristics, you can create a look that projects the required image by selecting the appropriate colours. Even a hint can make all the difference. The examples given apply mainly to western European society.

Approachable

The soft pinks, coral, peach and pastels. Warm colours that have a yellow base, for example tan, terracotta and rust.

Assertive

Strong colour contrast using blacks, greys or deep navy with bright or deep reds, berry colours, or rich purples and violets. Depending on the clothing style, these colours can also convey drama or glamour.

Authority

The high contrast of very dark tones worn with very light tones is perceived as having authority and control, for example police officers, traffic wardens and nursing sisters. All wear high contrast colours as uniform or quasi-uniform. Black and white, dark navy and white or cream, and cool colours such as blue-grey, navy and grey have authority.

Business-like

Traditionally the sombre blues, greys and deep black-browns are the colours of sobriety and hard work. The darker blues, indigo and navy represent logic and organization. For a conservative look, they work best teamed with whites or light neutrals. Accent colours can come from any part of the palette provided the pattern is not too wild. With the exception of brown, they are city, not country colours. They are seen as respectable, classic colours and are associated with business.

Communicator

The whole range of medium blues is well received by an audience. They flatter a wide variety of skin tones and look good on TV and a conference platform.

Creative

Bright, warm colours, complex colours, unusual or unexpected colour combinations, or a touch of unusual colouring in an otherwise staid ensemble.

Dynamic

A dynamic look is achieved through contrast, by wearing large areas of bright, vivid colours contrasted with dark colours, for example bright green, magenta or red worn with black will create drama.

Elegant

Deep, subdued and complex colours worn together suggest elegance and understatement, for example fir green, deep burgundy. This look is further enhanced by using texture instead of colour contrast for its effect.

Enthusiastic

Oranges and yellows are bright and open, not easily missed. They can appear juvenile, optimistic, creative or busy.

Sensitive

The artistic and intuitive colours lie in the purple, violet, lavender and periwinkle palette. Just a small touch of one of these colours softens an otherwise hard or over-formal look.

Negotiator

The deeper, softer range of the brown family, warm muted browns, warm beige, coffee and mushroom worn with any of the earth colours are comfortable and easy to relate to. Neutral greys have the same effect. Accenting with coral, brick or red or a colour from one of the turquoise or jade families avoids monotony.

Relaxed and informal

Blending colours of the same tone and similar colour family, allowing little dark/light contrast, looks informal and comfortable. A mixture of the soft medium-toned blues found in denim and chambray looks casual and relaxed. Herb and spice colours create a natural look. They work well in natural fibres and look good in the country. It can be difficult to create a business look using this kind of colour scheme as it appears too warm and earthy.

WHY DO WE WEAR CLOTHES ANYWAY?

'Why do we wear clothes?' is a simple question with a complex answer. In the British climate for most occupations we are expected to wear clothes all the time, except in bed or in the bath. We wear clothes to keep warm, to show how rich we are, to show off in front of friends; for a host of social, personal, rational, aesthetic or emotional reasons, and sometimes for no apparently practical reason at all. Whatever the reasons, most commentators agree that in the end, all our reasons will be to do with sex, status, utility or personal expression. Before we can draw up a satisfactory list of reasons why we join in the complex game of covering and decorating our bodies, we need to get back to basics and establish what makes us tick.

The psychology of clothing

Several studies have been made of human needs. Abraham Maslow, a humanist psychologist writing in 1954, developed a theory of a hierarchy of needs. Maslow described human need operating at five levels which he saw forming a wide-based triangle, with more people at the base of the triangle than at its apex.

1. *Survival needs.* At the broad base of the triangle are the needs for the basics of human existence: food, water, shelter, warmth, clean air, sex, excretion and shelter.

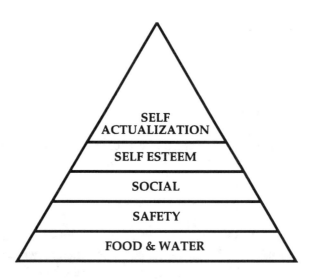

Figure 7.2 *Maslow's hierarchy of needs*

2. *Security needs.* The need to be safe; protected from danger and deprivation.
3. *Social needs.* The need to belong, to give and receive friendship and love, to enjoy social activities, to feel accepted.
4. *Ego needs.* The need for self-esteem, self-respect and the respect of others. A desire for autonomy, achievement and recognition, to have influence.
5. *Creative needs.* At the apex of the triangle is self-realization or self-actualization; needs are centred on self, personal growth and development in order to realize potential, to fulfil self.

Everyone has needs at levels one and two and so, if you are in work and your country is not at war, the basic needs of security and survival will have been met. Employment provides income, which provides food, shelter and security.

The needs to do with belonging, self-esteem and creativity at levels three, four and five are the ones that affect our projection of self through clothes. If you are reading this at the moment comfortably settled indoors with no prospect of a raging blizzard, dangerous plants, wild animals or enemy troops outside, you won't need clothes as protection from a hostile environment. Dress has little place at the basic levels of physiological need, so once you have satisfied the need for physical protection the way you decide to dress will arise from other factors closer to the apex of the triangle.

Twenty-one reasons why we wear clothes

Not much published research has been done since Flügel's *The Psychology of Clothes*, a major work from the 1930s. He suggested fundamental motives for wearing clothes. Most writers since then agree with him that our choice of clothes is to do with sex, status, display or utility.

Display

Display is about self-expression, creativity, aesthetics, expressing mood, feelings or personal style by decorating the body itself with scars, tattoos, nail varnish, hair, henna on palms of hands and soles of feet or covering the body with decoration in the form of clothes. In most social situations we do not see much of another's body except hands and face. We respond to display through the clothes, not the body.

129

Social correctness   Knowing what to wear at a wedding or an interview, we feel superior because we know the rules. Socially correct clothes can bind groups of people together and ostracize those who are not familiar with the etiquette.

To attract a partner of the appropriate sex   Displaying primary or secondary sexual characteristics is intended to attract a mate. Men's reproductive organs are conveniently sited outside the body, unlike women's. Female breasts can either be hidden, flattened or gift-wrapped. Secondary sexual characteristics in males are height, broad shoulders and shapely legs. For women it is the distinctive curve of waist and hip, displayed in different shapes according to current taste and fashion: robust to fragile, statuesque to pocket Venus, buxom to anorexic.

Most cultures agree that it is not effective to put all the goods on display at once.

The 'three tricks of sexual allure' have been described by C Willett Cunnington as:

Concealment. To provoke curiosity; a glimpse of stocking was something shocking.
Allusion. To provoke associated ideas; underwear as outerwear associated with undressing, simulated display of underwear as in lace camisole showing under a business suit.
Exposure. Which 'having provoked surprise soon passes into indifference'.

> I'm beginning to like this return to short skirts. I find it revives my memory for faces
>
> *Man About Town* 1929

To inspire envy in rivals of the same sex   To look richer, thinner or more interesting than possible rivals.

Modesty   The parts of your anatomy you are expected to cover up and the parts you are allowed to display vary from age to age, culture to culture and occasion to occasion. Exposing parts of the body need not be immodest or indecent within your own social and cultural traditions. Revealing parts of your person can arouse desire or disgust according to the variables of the social context, the reason for display, the age and desirability of the body in question, the kind of clothes being worn and the attitude and expectations of other people. At work today, primary sexual characteristics are kept hidden and secondary characteristics are hinted at but covered up. A woman who would wear a revealing décolletage to a charity ball would consider it bad taste to reveal chest or shoulders during the day in the office. The tight fit of Nick Kamen's jeans at the laundromat is rarely suitable for a board meeting.

Gender identity　　Early conditioning from family and school establishes the extent to which we perceive our masculinity or femininity. We are also influenced by powerful messages from popular culture about the definition of men and women through their dress. Films, TV and advertising help us to establish and recognize desirable models. As they shift, so do we in our desire to conform to or reject those role models. We all know quite clearly what constitutes male and female dress.

In 1986 a study at a Bowling Green State University, Ohio, showed that although women felt able to borrow freely from the male wardrobe, the same freedom was not available for men. Many clothing items, accessories and fabrics were considered to be female wear only.

The City Suit with its straight lines, sober cut and dark colours, represents a behavioural expectation of business and professional men. When the suit in its classic form pervades men's business dress, it is usually an indicator that professional and financial success, the traditionally masculine virtues, are socially valued. The 1950s and 1980s were times when professional success was emphasized. In the 1960s and 1970s and now in the 1990s concepts of masculinity have been challenged.

The traditional view of the uniform worn to express authority is exemplified by airline uniforms; commanding, powerful, male pilots wear quasi-military uniform of high-contrast dark jacket and trousers with white shirt and lots of braid. The nurturing, servicing female flight attendants wear the apron and heavy make up and stiff hair styles reminiscent of a geisha girl; a combination of waitress, nurse and mother. What will they do about appropriate uniforms when more men work inside the cabin and more women fly the planes?

Protection from magic and spirits

Folk-lore and legend are full of stories about items of clothing having magic properties. Tolkien's magic ring, seven league boots, the black in Harlequin's colourful costume which reminded his audience that he had the power to make things disappear.

For good luck

Today, even the most sensible of us trust to the properties of our 'lucky T-shirt' when sitting exams, the dark red paisley tie for sales presentations, wearing our knickers inside out to bring us luck at interviews. Athletes, actors and apprentices all have their talismans. Margaret Thatcher considered that the dark navy silk dress she wore during the Falklands year brought her good luck.

Protection against the general unfriendliness of the world

We use clothes as reassurance against lack of love. If cold can be equated with a lack of love, then clothes can be seen as a substitute for love. Mothers are always concerned that children should be warm enough, 'Have you got your jacket?', 'Are you wearing your vest?' When we feel comfortable and 'at home' in a social or business situation, we are prepared to take off our outer things. When we feel insecure we keep them on as a defence against real or imagined emotional hostility. Physical and emotional security can be gained from the comfort of feeling wrapped up tight.

The `Falling in Love Factor'

Some people experience a long-term love match between themselves and an item of clothing. My husband reluctantly got divorced from his first corduroy jacket after a 35-year relationship. Others experience a short but passionate affair with a jacket or a piece of jewellery that resulted from love at first sight, 'BUY ME, Buy me' it said. We bought it, loved it, discarded it and waited to be seduced again. In the words of the song:

Til it wilted I wore it, I'll always adore it, My sweet little Alice Blue Gown

Protection from moral danger

Colour. The dangers of an immoral world can be held at bay by careful choice of colour, particularly through the extremes of black and white. Black clothes can signify seriousness and sobriety. White clothes stand for innocence and purity, as symbolized in the wimple of a nun's habit. It follows that bright colours must indicate moral freedom and a frivolous nature.

Cover. If the body is a source of evil passions as much of it as possible should be covered so that the temptation is hidden. Muslim women cover themselves from head to foot.

Weight. Thick, heavy clothes can protect against physical dangers and, by association, from moral dangers.

Stiffness. Stiff clothes equate with moral uprightness and firmness. Loose clothes indicate a corresponding sloppy way of life.

Tightness. Tight clothes can be a symbol for moral control indicating firm personal control over passions and morality. Loose clothes were a self-indulgence as far as the Victorians were concerned. A loose robe worn in private was seen only by other women or lovers or was worn by invalids. To some minds a 'woman in a dressing gown' is a symbol of general disorder, an inability to manage the house and its needs.

Protection from the elements

The need to protect ourselves from heat, cold, rain, snow or heat-wave has resulted in the design of special garments such as the Burberry mac, which has a specific protective function.

Protection from a hostile environment

We can use clothes to protect us from dust, sand, thorns, nettles, pollution or design a form of body armour to protect us from our human enemies. Space suits and coveralls worn at nuclear power stations protect the wearers from hostile environments.

Group identity

Clothes can help us to recognize people who are like ourselves. This way we can recognize our enemies, seek peer group approval and be seen to belong to a professional group or social class. There is a need to be identified, to be seen to belong. For members of the Shaker community, the way they think and what they stand for is worn on their backs — piety and modesty made visible. Conforming through clothes means being a willing member of a team — whether it's a football team, corporate team or fund-raising fun-run, the same clothes mean shared values, goals and aspirations.

In large hospitals, group identity is shown through the dress of different hospital 'tribes' — physios, chiropodists, pharmacists, nursing staff, consultants, managers. However, all members of a given group will not look identical, even in uniform. Differences, not only in physical appearance but also in level of personal tidiness, cleanliness, degree of fit and flattery of outfit, posture, confidence, self-esteem and attitude, will make them appear different. Most social groups establish guide-lines for what is appropriate within their own boundaries. A certain degree of variety is allowed. Badges of office and other emblems are agreed between members of the group to show their allegiance to each other.

National identity Wearing special costumes not seen anywhere else is a sign of geographic location or nationality. In a business context if you wear national dress, do you know what messages will be picked up? Will they be the same as the ones you intended to transmit? I met an Asian doctor recently who worked in a family planning clinic. She often wears a sari because she feels she inspires trust in the women she sees by dressing as they do. When she has to address the Regional Health Authority about matters of local funding and research, she wonders whether the sober suited, predominantly male panel will see 'sari' before 'expert'. Will they presume that allegiance to ethnic tradition is more important than observation of local business etiquette? Will they see a refreshing alternative to dark-suited business women? Or will they just see a professional woman doing her job?

Fashion and anti-fashion Continuity and a belief in the status quo can be demonstrated through traditional clothing styles. Traditional or 'fixed' costume (anti-fashion) changes slowly. The whole point of 'modish' costume (fashion) is that it changes rapidly and constantly. Wearers of fashion are therefore showing their allegiance to modernity and change.

Occupation Carrying essential articles or tools of the trade are an indication of occupation, for example the sword and spurs of military dress uniform. The briefcase, tape measure and stethoscope are all clues to occupation.

It is the law Until the Offence Against the Persons Act 1894 is repealed, it is still against the law to appear in a public place without your clothes on.

Status Your status or your standing in the community or at work — whether you are more or less important than your colleague, neighbour, competitor, family member—can be demonstrated through clothes. Status is rewarded by trophies: the desire for a token of victory, a fur coat, a scalp, a Breitling watch or even a wife or toy boy. Certain special ornaments were always the prerogative of important citizens. The mayoral chain of office, the royal crown, orb and sceptre, military stripes, flashes and badges all denote rank. Professionals have their status symbols too: from watches to secretaries, Mercedes to Fiestas, whole buildings to helicopters.

Wealth

The 'conspicuous consumption' of Thorstein Veblen's *Theory of the Leisure Class* is most easily demonstrated through clothes and fashion, sumptuosity and carelessness. In societies where wealth is admired and is a means of obtaining power, the wealthy seek to be noticed. Consumerism in the form of clothes is one of the easiest ways to show that you've got what it takes. The simplest and most obvious way to demonstrate wealth is to hang as many valuable objects as you can about your person. The intention of Henry VIII and Charles II at the Field of the Cloth of Gold was to astonish and impress each other. There is a more subtle means of showing off, but it's only effective with those who share the same language. Understatement can be very powerful. An outfit of excellent cut and fit, made from good quality cloth in light neutral colours, demonstrates you have the time, money and good taste to shop for the best (as well as pay the dry cleaning bills). For greatest effect the materials used should ideally require labour-intensive production or be difficult to get hold of. Cashmere or trendy and environmentally friendly pineapple cloth might score some points too. Jewellery and precious stones have a long history as wealth indicators. Actual coinage or its equivalent not only shows that the wearer is rich but can make an immediate purchase of an object or service.

Clothes as a weapon

Clothes used as a form of terrorism can inspire fear. Punks, Hells Angels and armed robbers know the value of the threat of violence given by masks, weapons, chains, studs or leather. Today's fashionable élite have the same effect on ordinary people as the Court of Louis XIV had on French peasants. Luxury fabrics and grotesque styles emphasize the distance between them and the real world. There also exists a 'style mafia' who terrorize the conservative dresser, such as the young fashion writers who can give intellectual justification to what the rest of us don't understand. When the Japanese designers of the 1980s deconstructed garments so that the beauty of the fabric's essential nature was evident, they made the human form irrelevant except as a carrier. We said we didn't understand why, and the style mafia made us feel stupid.

I have a fantasy about running an Understanding the Language of

Clothes course at a business school along the same lines as a Finance for Non-Financial Managers course. At the advanced level, the nuances of sartorial style could be debated without a word being spoken. The intellectual temperature would be red hot. Witticisms would flash across the room without a word being spoken. As Peter York once remarked, 'Who said the art of conversation's dead when a man can make a point with his sock!'

FURTHER READING

Berne, Eric (1967) *Games People Play*, Penguin, London

Brennan, L and Block, D (1991) *The Complete Book of Business Etiquette*, Piatkus, London

Carnegie, Dale (1990) *How to Win Friends and Influence People*, Mandarin, London

Cunnington, Willett C (1948) *The Art of English Costume*, Collins, London

Davies, Philippa (1991) *Status*, Piatkus, London

Deal, T and Kennedy, A (1988) *Corporate Cultures: The Rites and Rituals of Corporate Life*, Penguin, London

Eggert, Max (1992) *The Perfect Interview: All You Need to Get It Right First Time*, Century, London

Flügel, J C (1930) *The Psychology of Clothes*, Hogarth Press, London

Goffman, Erving (1990) *The Presentation of Self in Everyday Life*, Penguin, London

Golzen, G and Garner, A (1990) *Smart Moves: Successful Strategies and Tactics for Career Management*, Basil Blackwell, Oxford

Handy, Charles B (1986) *Understanding Organisations*, Penguin, London

Hebdige, Dick (1990) *Sub-Culture: The Meaning of Style*, Routledge, London

Heylin, Angela (1991) *Putting it Across*, Michael Joseph, London

Hinton, Perry R (1993) *The Psychology of Interpersonal Perception*, Routledge, London

King, Norman (1987) *The First Five Minutes*, Simon & Schuster

Lancaster, Graham (1993) *The 20% Factor*, Kogan Page, London

Leeds, Dorothy (1991) *Marketing Yourself: How to Sell Yourself and Get the Jobs You've Always Wanted*, Piatkus, London

Lewis, David (1990) *The Secret Language of Success*, Bantam Books, London

Lurie, Alison (1992) *The Language of Clothes*, Bloomsbury, London

Maslow, Abraham H (1987) *Motivation and Personality*, Harper and Row, New York

McCormack, Mark H (1986) *What They Don't Teach You at Harvard Business School*, Fontana, London

McDowell, Colin (1992) *Dressed To Kill: Sex, Power, and Clothes*, Hutchinson, London

Molloy, John T (1975) *Dress For Success*, Peter H Wyden, New York

Morea, Peter (1990) *Personality: Introduction to the Theories of Psychology*, Penguin, London

Naisbitt, J and Aburdene, P (1991) *Megatrends 2000*, Pan, London

Polhemus, T and Proctor, L (1978) *Fashion and Anti-Fashion*, Thames and Hudson, London

Rein, I J, Kotler, P and Stoller, M R (1987) *High Visibility: How Executives, Politicians, Entertainers, Athletes and other Professionals Create, Market and Achieve Successful Images*, Heinemann, London

Rosencrantz, Mary Lou (1972) *Clothing Concepts: A Social Psychological Approach*, Macmillan, New York

Sarch, Yvonne (1992) *How To Be Head-Hunted: How to Make Yourself the Best Person for the Job*, Business Books, London

Segerman-Peck, Lily (1991) *Networking and Mentoring: A Women's Guide*, Piatkus, London

Seitz, Victoria A (1992) *Your Executive Image*, Bob Adams, Holbrook, MA, USA

Willis, L and Daisley, J (1990) *Springboard: Women's Development Workbook*, Kogan Page, London

Wilson, Elizabeth (1985) *Adorned in Dreams: Fashion and Modernity*, Virago, London

York, Peter (1984) *Modern Times*, Heinemann, London

INDEX

POSITIVE IMAGE COURSES

For further information about Eleri
Sampson and the courses she runs on
communication and effective
self-presentation skills for companies and
individuals, please telephone:

081-675 5806